Vouchers, Class Size Reduction, and Student Achievement
CONSIDERING THE EVIDENCE

by Alex Molnar

Phi Delta Kappa Educational Foundation
Bloomington, Indiana U.S.A.

Cover design by Victoria Voelker

Phi Delta Kappa Educational Foundation
408 North Union Street
Post Office Box 789
Bloomington, Indiana 47402-0789
U.S.A.

Printed in the United States of America

Library of Congress Catalog Card Number 00-101823
ISBN 0-87367-829-X

TABLE OF CONTENTS

VOUCHERS

In the early 1870s, demoralized by their crushing defeat in the Franco-Prussian War, many French citizens angrily blamed the public school system for their woes. They declared that it was "the Prussian teacher [who] has won the war."[1]

To improve the schools, and presumably France's prospects in the next war, a French parliamentary commission in 1872 recommended a religious school voucher plan remarkably similar to the ones currently being proposed in the United States. In 19th century France, however, hostility to the idea of providing public money to church schools was so widespread that the French Assembly never took up the plan.

Just over 100 years later, with the U.S. trade deficit at record levels, the authors of *A Nation at Risk* declared that America was headed for a disastrous defeat in a global economic war.[2] As in 19th century France, the public schools were called to account. *A Nation at Risk* helped make the belief that the U.S. system of public education is a catastrophic failure an article of faith in the nation's school reform deliberations. In so doing it helped set the stage for school voucher proposals in the late 1980s and 1990s.

Until the 1980s, the constitutional prohibition against church-state entanglements, public opposition to the use of tax funds for religious schools, and a lack of a generally available alternatives to public schools kept voucher proposals on the fringes of American school reform.

Education vouchers were first proposed in the United States in 1955 by economist Milton Friedman.[3] Friedman argued for providing parents with vouchers and allowing them to choose any school, public or private, for their children to attend. In his view, an education market would be more efficient at allocating education resources than would a system of government-run schools. Friedman's idea initially drew scant attention and little support.

The private school choice plans proposed in the United States in the late 1950s and early 1960s were not motivated by a desire to create competition and an education market. These plans grew out of opposition to court-ordered desegregation in the wake of the 1954 U.S. Supreme Court's *Brown* v. *Board of Education* decision.[4] The Virginia legislature in 1956 passed a "tuition-grant" program and in 1960 a "scholarship" plan that provided students with tax dollars to pay the tuition at any qualified nonsectarian school in their district. The Virginia laws and other "freedom of choice" plans passed by Southern legislatures expressly sought to help maintain segregated school systems.

Since the late 1950s, private school choice has moved steadily toward the mainstream of the school reform debate. Private school vouchers have found support primarily among three groups:

1. Catholics who see taxpayer-financed vouchers as a fiscal lifeline for their cash-poor schools (some Catholics remain opposed to vouchers because they fear that public funding will increase public regulation of religious schools).
2. Free-market advocates who regard vouchers as a way of increasing efficiency in the provision of public education.
3. People of all political persuasions who, for various reasons, are dissatisfied with the shortcomings of what David Tyack, a historian of public education, has labeled "the one best system."[5]

In the late 1960s, the Democratic administration of President Lyndon Johnson embraced the idea of vouchers. At the time, the voucher constituency included not only some political conserva-

2

tives and segments of the business community, but also "de-schoolers" influenced by the writing of Ivan Illich,[6] progressive and black nationalist "free schoolers,"[7] social critics of the public education bureaucracy such as Paul Goodman,[8] and liberal academics such as Christopher Jencks.[9] The chance to craft "regulated" voucher plans — ensuring that the poorest recipients get the largest vouchers — appealed to many liberals.

The administration of President Richard Nixon subsequently advanced the Johnson proposal. However, little local enthusiasm emerged for the idea. Minneapolis, Rochester, Kansas City, Milwaukee, Gary, and Seattle all rejected the opportunity to participate. Only Alum Rock, California, tried the voucher plan, implementing it in the public school system with disappointing results and subsequently abandoning it.[10]

In 1971, the Panel on Non-Public Education of the Nixon Administration's Presidential Commission on School Finance proposed "parochiaid," which would have provided public money to religious schools. In the same year, the Supreme Court raised the legal barriers to government support for church schools. It held 8-0 in *Lemon v. Kurtzman* that distribution of tax dollars to private schools had to meet all of the following three tests to be constitutional: its purpose is secular, its main effect is to neither advance nor inhibit religion, and it does not excessively entangle the state with religion.[11]

Although "parochiaid" died for lack of sufficient political support and the threat that it would be ruled unconstitutional, the idea of spending tax dollars on education at church-affiliated private schools remained alive. Indeed, the "parochiaid" debate rehearsed many of the current arguments over private school vouchers and their use to pay tuition at religious schools.[12]

In 1983, 1985, and 1986, the Reagan Administration tried unsuccessfully to move voucher legislation through Congress. By turning the federal government's means-tested Chapter 1 program into an individual voucher program, the 1985 effort sought to re-establish the link between vouchers and "empowering" the poor, which had attracted liberals in the 1960s and 1970s.[13]

3

Choice Enters the Mainstream

According to George Washington University Professor Jeffrey Henig, with free-market arguments for private school vouchers meeting with no success, the administration of President Reagan shifted the discussion to public school choice.[14] This new emphasis broadened support for school "choice," which many now saw as a strategy to reform, rather than to dismantle, the public school system. Furthermore, supporters often associated choice with educational excellence and racial equity through its link to the popular magnet school concept. Many school districts had established magnet schools to promote school integration and as an alternative to court-ordered busing. Magnet schools offered a diverse array of innovative curricula to attract voluntary transfers to integrated schools. By shifting the focus from private school vouchers to public school choice, President Reagan successfully separated education choice from its racist and sectarian roots.[15]

Over the next eight years, beginning with Minnesota in 1988, 14 states enacted public school choice laws.[16] These laws allowed students to choose to attend any public school in the state that had room for them.

The idea of private school vouchers took the national stage again during the presidency of George Bush. Between 1990 and 1992, President Bush sent Vice President Dan Quayle to Oregon to speak on behalf of a voucher ballot initiative in that state. Bush expressed strong (and well-publicized) support for Wisconsin's 1990 private school voucher law, included "parental choice" in his 1991 "America 2000" reform initiative, and, in 1992, proposed a voucher plan he called a "G.I. Bill for Children."[17] Bush's Democratic challenger, Bill Clinton, took over the Reagan Administration's "public school choice" position during the 1992 presidential campaign.

At the state level, private school vouchers have been vigorously debated for 20 years. Since 1978, four states have held referenda on voucher plans: Michigan (1978), Oregon (1990), Colorado (1992), and California (1993). Each of these efforts failed by

4

approximately a 2-to-1 margin. California voters also rejected "regulated" voucher plans in 1980 and 1982 ballot initiatives.[18]

In 1993, Puerto Rico passed legislation that provided vouchers worth $1,500 per child that low-income families could use to send their children to any school, public or private (including religious schools that would accept them). The Puerto Rico Supreme Court struck down the private school portion of the bill in 1994.

Despite repeated setbacks, voucher legislation continues to be introduced in state legislatures and, since 1994, at the federal level.

The Battle Over Vouchers Today

Proponents of vouchers today base their position on three widely held views about public education: that education outcomes have deteriorated, that American public education costs have accelerated unreasonably, and that the public schools cannot reform themselves because of bureaucratic and political constraints.

Each of these beliefs is subject to serious challenge. There is considerable evidence that education outcomes actually have improved over the last 20 years. A 1993 report written by scientists at the Sandia National Laboratories found that U.S. public education performance was improving.[19] Between the 1970s and 1990, according to a 1994 RAND study, reading and math scores rose significantly for Hispanics and African Americans.[20] In a March 1998 article, Princeton University economist Alan Krueger reported that National Assessment of Educational Progress (NAEP) exams reveal rising American public school performance over the past 20 years.[21] For example, a student scoring in the 50th percentile today performs as well as the 56th-percentile student 25 years ago.[22] The most disadvantaged students have made the greatest gains. Moreover, between the early 1970s and 1990, the black-white NAEP test-score gap for 17-year-olds decreased by almost half (before increasing slightly in the 1990s).[23]

Contrary to the second widely held perception driving support for vouchers, Richard Rothstein and Karen Hawley Mills found that resources for regular classrooms at public schools have increased only modestly over the last several decades.[24] Rothstein and Mills reached this conclusion by identifying expenditures on special education, transportation, and other activities outside the regular classroom. In a survey of nine school districts, they found that inflation-adjusted per-pupil spending for regular education rose by only 28% from 1967 to 1991. In Los Angeles, inflation-adjusted per-pupil spending on regular education declined by 3.5% over the same period. If this decline in spending for regular education typifies developments in urban areas, it may help explain worsening relative academic outcomes in some urban public schools. Rothstein and Mills' research also suggests that carefully targeted increases in spending on regular classroom instruction in urban areas may increase both parental satisfaction and student achievement.

Of course, national statistics about gradually improving performance and the stagnation of funds flowing to regular classrooms in urban school districts are of little comfort to parents convinced that their own children will not get the lift they need from the local public school.

Parents who want better school for their kids *now* have been a receptive audience for the third widely held belief that underlies support for vouchers today: that public schools are incapable of reforming themselves because of bureaucratic and political constraints. This argument gained intellectual legitimacy with the 1990 publication of *Politics, Markets, and America's Schools* by John Chubb and Terry Moe.[25] In their book, Chubb and Moe argued that private school vouchers are needed because private schools exhibit superior academic performance and because public school performance has not improved despite reforms instituted during the 1980s.[26]

Chubb and Moe's claims notwithstanding, the research literature contains no clear evidence that private schools are better than public schools. Moreover, since most of the studies in the literature on public versus private schools use data for secondary schools, they are of limited value in predicting the impact of voucher programs that, for the most part, involve private elementary schools. (For a summary of the literature on public versus private schools, see pages 8 and 9.)

Many proponents of private school vouchers, such as Wisconsin Assembly member Annette "Polly" Williams, author of the Milwaukee Parental Choice Program legislation, link vouchers to their desire to empower poor families and raise the academic achievement of poor children. They argue that vouchers may improve achievement by forcing the public schools to compete in an education marketplace in which poor parents hold the power of the purse. What does the research evidence show?

The Milwaukee Parental Choice Voucher Program

Private school vouchers have been debated at the state level for more than 20 years. However, voucher legislation has become law in only three states: Wisconsin (1990), Ohio (1995), and Florida (1999).

Wisconsin established the country's first publicly funded private school voucher program in Milwaukee. Today, the Milwaukee Parental Choice Program (MPCP) is the voucher program for which the greatest volume of systematic data is available.

The MPCP initially allowed up to 1% of low-income Milwaukee Public School students (about 1,000 students) to attend participating private, nonsectarian schools within the city (see Table 1 on page 10). The program defined "low-income" as below 175% of the official U.S. poverty line. Each child attending a private school in the program receives a voucher worth the per-pupil equalized state aid to the Milwaukee Public Schools, originally set at $2,446 and currently $5,106 (in 1999-2000). The Wisconsin legislation that created Milwaukee's Choice program provided for yearly evaluations of the academic achievement of students attending Choice schools.

Participating schools had to meet only one of four requirements:

- At least 70% of pupils advance one grade level each year;
- Attendance averages at least 90%;
- At least 80% of students demonstrate significant academic progress; or
- At least 70% of their families meet parental involvement criteria established by the private school.

Public Versus Private Schools

Studies both support and refute the premise that private schools are better at producing high-achieving students. Evans and Schwab, for example, found overall positive effects from attending Catholic schools, while Goldhaber found no advantage to private school attendance.*

One of the most contentious issues in this research literature is the issue of selection bias, that is, whether differences in achievement are explained on the basis of who attends private schools. The unrepresentative set of private schools in one widely used database of private schools (High School and Beyond) is also of concern.

In a recent study, David Figlio and Joe Stone of the University of Oregon drew on the National Education Longitudinal Survey and a Dun and Bradstreet directory of private schools to analyze public and private school performance in eighth- to 12th-grade math and science.** Their research attempts to simulate the placement of otherwise equivalent students into different school environments and thereby to isolate the achievement effect of attendance at a public versus private school. Figlio and Stone caution that their results on the performance of low-income and low-achievement students are based on very small numbers (47 low-income students and 39 low-achieving students).

Figlio and Stone's study reveals the complexity of the issue of private versus public school performance and the danger of drawing simplistic, sweeping conclusions about the relative performance of public and private schools. Figlio and Stone estimate either no achievement effect or negative effects overall for attendance at a religious school. However, they find that African-American and Hispanic students who attend religious schools outperform their public school counterparts, especially in urban areas. According to Figlio and Stone, nonreligious private schools have a positive effect on math and science achievement primarily for low-income and initially low-achieving students. High-achieving students may do less well in science in private nonreligious schools.

Figlio and Stone advise that their findings should be used very carefully if deployed in the debate about vouchers. As they explain, their estimated effects only simulate what would happen if a few students moved from private to public schools. In this situation, when low-income and initially low-achieving students attend private schools, these students may benefit from changes in who is in school with them – "peer group composition." What Figlio and Stone cannot estimate is the effect on achievement that would occur if larger numbers of students moved from public to private schools. Large-scale implementation of vouchers could have negative achievement effects in both public and private schools because of the changes in student body composition it could produce.

On the whole, the research literature gives no clear guidance as to whether private schools are better at producing desired education outcomes than are public schools. Since most of the studies use data for secondary schools, they are of limited value in understanding the impact of voucher programs that involve elementary schools.

---

*William N. Evans and Robert M. Schwab, "Finishing High School and Starting College: Do Catholic Schools Make a Difference?" *Quarterly Journal of Economics* 110 (November 1995): 941-74. See also, James S. Coleman, Thomas Hoffer, and Sally Kilgore, *High School Achievement: Public, Catholic, and Private Schools Compared* (New York: Basic Books, 1982). Dan D. Goldhaber, "Public and Private High School: Is School Choice an Answer to the Productivity Problem?" *Economics of Education Review* 15 (April 1996): 99-109.
**David N. Figlio and Joe A. Stone, "School Choice and Student Performance: Are Private Schools Really Better?" Discussion Paper 1141-97 (Madison, Wis.: Institute for Research on Poverty, September 1997).

Table 1. Milwaukee Parental Choice Program Profile, 1990-1999.

School Year	Number of Schools	Number of Applications	Average # of Voucher Students*	Voucher Amount	Total Cost of Vouchers (millions)	Annual Attrition Rate
1990-1991	7	577	300	$2,446	$0.73	0.46
1991-1992	6	689	512	$2,643	$1.35	0.35
1992-1993	11	998	594	$2,745	$1.63	0.31
1993-1994	12	1,049	704	$2,985	$2.10	0.27
1994-1995	12	1,046	771	$3,209	$2.47	0.28
1995-1996	17	†	1288	$3,667	$4.61	†
1996-1997	20	†	1616	$4,373	$7.07	†
1997-1998	23	†	1497	$4,696	$7.03	†
1998-1999	88 ‡	†	5806 **	$4,894	$28.41 **	†

* Calculated as the average of September and January memberships, plus summer school membership.
** Estimate.
† Information was not kept by the state.
‡ Three schools are within one organization: Seeds of Health.

Sources: State of Wisconsin Department of Public Instruction web page, http://www.dpi.state.wi.us/dpi/ dfm/sms/histmem.html; and John F. Witte, Troy D. Sterr, and Christopher A. Thorn, *Fifth-Year Report: Milwauke Parental Choice Program* (Madison: Robert M. LaFollette Institute of Public Affairs, University of Wisconsin-Madison, December 1995).

Unlike public schools, teachers at Choice schools need not be certified, nor does the curriculum of the schools have to be reviewed or accredited by an outside agency. Choice schools do not have to meet the financial disclosure or other record-keeping requirements placed on the public schools. And as the result of a lawsuit, participating private schools need not serve children with exceptional needs.

The Wisconsin legislature created Milwaukee's Choice program as a five-year experiment and provided for yearly evaluations of the academic achievement of students attending Choice schools. Governor Thompson vetoed the five-year time limit on the program but left the requirement of annual program evaluations intact. The Wisconsin Supreme Court upheld the constitutionality of the Wisconsin law in 1992, reasoning that it affected a small number of children living in poverty, that it did not include religious schools, and that what the state learned from the experience might benefit children elsewhere in Wisconsin.[27]

The Milwaukee Parental Choice Program was modified in 1993 (effective 1994-95) to raise the number of students who could participate from 1% to 1.5% of the Milwaukee Public School population (that is, to about 1,500 students). A 1995 change allowed religious schools to participate in the MPCP and raised the eligibility ceiling to 7% of the Milwaukee Public School enrollment in 1995-96 and 15% (about 15,000 students) in 1996-97.

The 1995 revision of the MPCP, deemed constitutional by the Wisconsin Supreme Court on 10 June 1998, does *not* require that the schools participating in the program gather the achievement data necessary for a comprehensive evaluation. Because the necessary data are unavailable, no evaluation of the achievement effect of the program has been conducted since 1995. Although the Wisconsin Legislative Audit Bureau is required to issue a report in the year 2000, no meaningful evaluation of the achievement effect of the program is likely in the future unless the legislation authorizing the program is amended to require an evaluation.

Since 1990 there have been five official yearly evaluations of the Milwaukee voucher experiment (discussed at length in the next section) by University of Wisconsin political science Professor John Witte.[28] Witte found no statistically significant differences between the achievement of students attending Choice schools and the achievement of random samples of students attending the Milwaukee Public Schools. However, he did find a high degree of parental satisfaction with Choice schools.

A 1995 report by Harvard Professor Paul Peterson sharply criticized Witte and his statistical methods.[29] Peterson argued that Witte's methods understated the positive academic impact of the Milwaukee Parental Choice Program. Peterson's argument echoed a 1992 critique, *The Milwaukee Parental Choice Program*, written by George Mitchell for the Wisconsin Policy Research Institute.[30]

In February 1995 the Wisconsin Legislative Audit Bureau, the research arm of the legislature, released its own report on the Milwaukee program. The report did not find Witte's methods inappropriate. However, it contended that no conclusion — not even Witte's finding of no significant difference — could be drawn about academic performance under the voucher program compared to the Milwaukee Public Schools.[31]

During the 1995 legislative debate over the expansion of the Choice program, the Peterson critique and the Witte annual reviews enabled both advocates and opponents to claim that the data supported their position. Unfortunately, instead of attempting to strengthen and improve the evaluation requirements for the Milwaukee Parental Choice Program, voucher supporters lobbied successfully to eliminate the annual program evaluation requirement. As revised in 1995 (Act 27), the evaluation components of the MPCP consisted of a requirement that the Legislative Audit Bureau report on the finances and performance of the program after five years (due 15 January 2000) and a provision requiring that each voucher school provide the Wisconsin Department of Public Instruction with an annual independent financial audit. However, the 1995 revision of the MPCP did not require that the schools participating in the program gather the achievement data necessary for a rigorous evaluation.

The 1995 legislation allowed religious schools to participate in the program and raised the number of students who could participate to 7% of the Milwaukee Public School enrollment in 1995-96 and 15% in 1996-97. The new legislation also allowed up to 100% of the students attending a Choice school to be voucher students.

The Debate Over the Achievement Effect
of the Milwaukee Voucher Program

Three research teams have analyzed the data collected during the first four years of the Milwaukee voucher program.

- University of Wisconsin-Madison political science Professor John Witte is the principal author of each of the first four annual evaluations of the program. He and his team are the only researchers to have analyzed fifth-year data on the program.[32] In a January 1997 paper, Witte summarized the findings of his first four evaluations and presented a reanalysis of some of his data in light of criticisms of his methods and findings. In addition, Witte published a synthesis of his findings in 1998.[33]

- In August 1996 and March 1997, Professors Jay Greene (University of Houston), Paul Peterson (Harvard), and Jiangtao Du (Harvard) issued two reanalyses of Witte's data on the first four years of the program.[34]

- In September 1997, Princeton Professor Cecilia Rouse released a paper, subsequently published in the *Quarterly Journal of Economics*, that analyzes the achievement data from the Choice program's first four years. In December 1997, Rouse published a paper comparing performance in three categories of schools within the MPS system, both to each other and to the Choice schools.[35]

In considering the research designs and findings of Witte; Greene, Peterson, and Du; and Rouse, it is useful to understand the Milwaukee Parental Choice Program's scope and character. The program has never involved a large number of students and has never reached the total enrollment authorized by law. Nonetheless, some students have been turned away because the school they wished to attend had no space at their grade level. According to the Wisconsin Legislative Audit Bureau's 1995 report, 30.3% of the children enrolled in the program one year do not return the next year.[36]

The MPCP overwhelmingly supports elementary school students. According to the 1995 Legislative Audit Bureau Report, 23.2% of the participants in the Milwaukee voucher program in 1994-95 enrolled in kindergarten, 61.1% in kindergarten through third grade, and 76% in kindergarten through fifth grade.[37] None of the evaluations of the Milwaukee program contain data on high school students because so few voucher students attend high school.

For 1999-2000 an MPCP voucher equals $5,106.[38] The Milwaukee Public Schools also provide transportation for those voucher students who require it. The voucher compares with a per-pupil expenditure in the Milwaukee Public Schools of $7,869 for 1997-98. (As well as the state support that sets the voucher amount, MPS total spending per pupil includes funding from local tax revenues, federal aid, and private sources.) Of the $7,869 total, on average, elementary (K-6) schools directly received $3,875 per-pupil, K-8 schools received $4,234, middle schools $4,831, and high schools $4,659 per pupil. In addition, schools also received money for special education. Money not distributed directly to the schools is used for capital improvements, recreation programs, alternative education programs, food service, building maintenance, transportation, and other central support services. Central administration costs account for approximately 5% or less of the Milwaukee budget.[39]

In sum, while Brent Staples in *The New York Times* claimed on 4 January 1998 that vouchers are limited to $3,000 and are less than half what public schools spend per pupil, neither statement is true.[40] Indeed, since Choice students fall primarily in the relatively inexpensive primary grades, vouchers usually exceed what most MPS schools receive directly for pupils in the same grades. It is impossible to judge whether voucher schools or public schools have more resources in Milwaukee because information is lacking on what participating private schools receive from private sources and because the range of services offered by private and public schools differs (private schools, for example, need not provide special education).

Another problem with interpreting the data is that three schools, Bruce Guadalupe, Harambee, and Urban Day, enrolled more than 80% of all voucher students in the first four years of the program.[41] Each of these schools had a long history and established reputation prior to the Milwaukee voucher program. This makes it difficult to generalize to large-scale voucher programs that would require many new schools.

Yet another problem with generalizing data from the Milwaukee experience to predict the effectiveness of large-scale voucher programs is that Milwaukee parents who send their children to voucher schools may be quite distinct from Milwaukee parents who do not apply for the program. Although about 60,000 students are eligible for the program, only a relatively small number apply to Choice schools each year (see Table 1). The program may be attracting a small subset of low-income parents with distinctive characteristics. In his evaluations, John Witte found that, when compared to Milwaukee Public School parents, parents who send their children to voucher schools are better educated and more involved in their children's education, have higher academic expectations, and are more critical of the Milwaukee Public Schools.[42] These findings have not been disputed. This suggests that MPCP parents are so-called high-voice parents.

To determine the academic impact of the Milwaukee voucher program, all of the researchers whose work is described here use the same test data from the Iowa Test of Basic Skills in reading and math.

Why Different Researchers Reach Different Conclusions

When researchers in ideologically polarized debates disagree, general readers who want to weigh the "facts" for themselves can end up confused. To avoid this problem, this section walks the reader through the findings of the three efforts to analyze the Milwaukee experience. It seeks to explain in everyday language how essentially the same underlying data can lead different analysts to different conclusions.

There is actually less disagreement than meets the eye between the findings of the three Milwaukee evaluations. When researchers of the MPCP program use similar methods, they come to the same basic conclusions.

Researchers of the Milwaukee voucher program arrive at conflicting results for two basic reasons: 1) they use different definitions of the reference or control group to which the performance of voucher program participants should be compared, and 2) they use different methods to control for family background and student ability. All of the researchers must contend with the relatively small samples of students in the databases analyzed. All must address the shrinkage (or "attrition") of their sample due to student mobility and missing data. All of them also lack any model of what actually goes on in schools or of the educational features (such as small class size or an innovative curriculum) that may generate good outcomes.

Following, in summary, is what the research on the Milwaukee Parental Choice Program tells us.

- Disagreement exists about whether the voucher program generates positive outcomes compared to the Milwaukee Public School (MPS) system. Two of three research teams think no positive outcomes result in reading. Two of three teams think that positive outcomes result in math.

- The evaluations all deal with small samples. Many students drop out of the experiment, possibly on a nonrandom basis. These data deficiencies should be kept in mind when interpreting the results.[43]

- The parents of voucher applicants have more education and higher expectations than parents of most Milwaukee Public School students. Wherever they attend school, the children of such parents may improve over time compared to other students.

- Students in a group of public schools with small classes outperform Choice students (according to the only analysis that looks at different groups within the MPS system).

- Lacking the necessary data, the evaluations cannot look at the education process inside the Choice schools. They can not explain what lies behind any differences in performance between Choice and MPS schools or among the Choice schools.

- More than 80% of Milwaukee voucher students attended three schools with established reputations. At best, the experiment tells us something about how these particular private schools compare with Milwaukee public schools, as a group. It indicates nothing about the impact of larger-scale voucher programs.

The Cleveland Scholarship and Tutoring Program

Ohio enacted the Cleveland Scholarship and Tutoring Program (CSTP) legislation in March 1995. (Table 2 profiles the program.)[44] The CSTP legislation allowed the Ohio Superintendent of Public Instruction to create a pilot voucher program in Cleveland. The Cleveland program is supported largely by money from Ohio's Disadvantaged Pupil Impact Aid Program, previously earmarked for the Cleveland Public Schools.

Scholarship recipients are selected by lottery, with priority going to applicants whose family income is less than the federal poverty level. Second priority goes to families whose income is less than twice the poverty level. There is no income cap on participation.

The approximately 30,000 K-3 students who reside within the Cleveland School District are eligible to apply to the program. Once admitted to the program, students may receive scholarships through eighth grade.

Since the Cleveland voucher program allows religious schools to participate, its constitutionality was immediately challenged. On 31 July 1996 the Franklin County Court of Common Pleas held the program constitutional and allowed it to be implemented. On 1 May 1997 an Ohio appeals court ruled the program unconstitutional. In May 1999 the Ohio Supreme Court struck down the program on procedural grounds, ruling that the program was unconstitutional for the way in which the legislature ap-

Table 2. Cleveland Scholarship and Tutoring Program Profile, 1996-1999.*

School Year	Number of Schools	Number of Applications	Number of Voucher Students**	Average Value of Voucher	Total Cost of Vouchers (millions)	Annual Attrition Rate
1996-1997	56	6,244	1,994	$1,750	$3.18	17%
1997-1998	57	6,811	1,289	$1,776	$4.74	14%
1998-1999	60	4,429	1,320	N/A	N/A	N/A

* Includes figures only for the voucher component of the program, not the tutoring component.
** As of June for each school year.

Source: Ohio Department of Education.

proved the bill that founded the program, not for First Amendment reasons. The program was subsequently reauthorized by the legislature for two more years.[45]

Soon after the reauthorization, a new challenge to the CSTP was filed by the Ohio Education Association and others on First Amendment grounds in federal court. On 24 August 1999, federal judge Solomon Oliver ruled that the program was unconstitutional and ordered the voucher students to return to public schools for the 1999-2000 school year. After public outcry regarding the timing of the ruling, Judge Oliver allowed the currently enrolled voucher students to remain in the program for the fall 1999 semester.[46]

The case immediately was appealed to the 6th Circuit Court of Appeals in Cincinnati, where it is being reviewed. A decision is expected by the end of the 1999-2000 school year. Regardless of the appellate court's ruling, the case is expected to reach the U.S. Supreme Court.

On 24 June 1997 Professor Paul Peterson of Harvard issued a press release that some observers interpreted to mean that his research team was conducting the official evaluation of the Cleveland program. In fact, his study was privately funded, not commissioned by the Ohio Department of Education.

Three months later, in September, Peterson and co-authors Jay Greene and William Howell released a report that analyzed test scores from two private schools, Hope Central Academy and Hope Ohio City Academy. The achievement results were expressed as percentile-rank changes on fall-to-spring (1996-97) testing. Peterson, Greene, and Howell report overall K-3 percentile-rank changes of +5.6 (reading), -4.5 (language), +11.6 (math total), and +12.8 (math concepts). However, students in most schools gain every spring and fall back the next autumn. Indeed, as Peterson, Greene, and Howell report in a subsequent paper, by fall 1997 no significant gains for Hope students were observed in language. Significant gains were still observed in total math and reading scores.[47] More important, for changes in test scores to be meaningful, a carefully chosen comparison group also must be tested. Peterson, Greene, and Howell's September analysis had no such comparison group. Instead, it made a comparison to low-income Milwaukee voucher applicants whose results were not from the same test used by the Hope schools. Their September 1997 evaluation is so flawed that it contributes little, if anything, to an understanding of how voucher programs might affect student achievement.

Official Evaluation Results for CSTP

The legislatively mandated, independent evaluation of the Cleveland Scholarship and Tutoring Program is being conducted by an Indiana University research team headed by Professor Kim Metcalf. This team published reports on the program's first year (1996-97) in March 1998 and on the second year (1997-98) in November 1998.[48]

To evaluate the Cleveland voucher program, Metcalf's team compared the test scores of third-grade voucher recipients with those of Cleveland Public School students, controlling for prior test scores and family characteristics. In 1996-97, the Metcalf evaluation examined third-grade performance because that was the lowest grade for which usable test data (from second grade) existed to measure student ability prior to the voucher experiment.

The first-year official evaluation report found that, after controlling for background characteristics, third-graders participating in the voucher program did not achieve at a higher level (on reading, language, mathematics, science, and social studies tests) than did students who remained in the Cleveland Public Schools. The second-year report (1997-98) found that fourth-grade students in the voucher program achieved significantly better than their public school counterparts in science and language. When classroom variables (for example, class size, teacher experience, and teacher level of education) are accounted for, the voucher students achieved significantly higher scores only in language.

The Peterson team criticize the Metcalf team's first-year report for several reasons.[49] They argue against the use of second-grade test data as a control for student performance prior to the voucher program on the ground that these test results "lack plausibility." They deem these test scores implausible because the scores showed the children of low-income, largely single-parent families performing close to the national average in the second grade and then scoring at substantially lower levels the next year. They also maintain that the second-grade test scores have implausibly weak correlations with family background characteristics. However, leaving out the second-grade test scores means that any comparison of voucher student achievement with that of public school students takes no account of differences in student performance prior to the program. Moreover, if the second-grade test scores were uniformly inflated for both voucher students and those who remained in the Cleveland Public Schools (for example, because second-grade public schools "teach to the test"), they still would be a good control measure.

Peterson, Greene, and Howell also maintain that the Metcalf evaluation team should have included student scores from the Hope schools, since 25% of voucher students went to these newly created schools. Metcalf's team had excluded the Hope schools because their students took a different test than did the public school students and students at other voucher schools. An additional problem with including Hope students is that approximately 58 of the 155 Hope students tested in the spring of 1996 appear not to have been tested in the fall of 1997, an unusually high attrition rate. Without information on the characteristics of these students, it cannot be known what effect their absence may have had on the reported results.

When Peterson, Greene, and Howell reanalyzed the official data excluding the second-grade test scores and including the Hope students with converted scores, they found that voucher students scored significantly higher in language and science, but not significantly higher in math, reading, or social studies. When the second-grade test scores were included, the Peterson team found results consistent with those of the official evaluation team: voucher students did not score significantly higher than their public school counterparts at conventional levels of statistical significance. Using a lower statistical significance threshold than conventional (the 0.10 level, a 10% chance that the results could have occurred by chance), they found that voucher students did better in language and science, but not in reading, math, and social studies.

The Metcalf team's second-year (1997-98) evaluation also found that not all schools participating in the voucher program had similar achievement results. Students attending established private schools were responsible for the voucher student achievement advantage in science and language. Students in the newly established, private Hope schools scored significantly lower than their public school counterparts in all tested areas.

The finding that student performance in the new voucher schools is significantly worse than student performance in public schools raises serious questions about the viability of voucher programs as a large-scale education reform. Existing private schools may produce benefits for low-income students by placing them with a majority of students from more privileged or more academically oriented backgrounds. However, the adoption of large-scale voucher programs may alter the social context that produces whatever achievement benefit there may be for low-income minority students attending private schools.[50]

Private Voucher Programs

Voucher programs supported by private sources provide another potential source of information on the educational consequences of vouchers. In 1998-99 there were 41 privately funded voucher programs in the United States, according to Troy Williamson of the CEO America Foundation (interview, 29 March 1999). There have been few systematic efforts to study the effect these programs are having on student achievement. This section describes those programs for which achievement data exist or for which an evaluation plan that will provide achievement information has been adopted.

Milwaukee. Perhaps the country's largest private program operates in Milwaukee. Partners Advancing Values in Education

(PAVE) — formerly the Milwaukee Archdiocesan Education Foundation — was founded in 1992. PAVE provides low-income families with scholarships worth half of the tuition charged by a private religious or nonsectarian school up to a maximum of $1,000 for elementary and middle school students and $1,500 for high school students. PAVE's major donors include the Lynde and Harry Bradley Foundation, TREK Corporation, CEO America, Johnson Controls, Northwestern Mutual Life Insurance Co., Siebert Lutheran Foundation, and Wisconsin Electric Power.

Of the five evaluations of the PAVE program, only the 1994 report made a serious effort to determine the program's effect on student achievement.[51] The 1994 evaluation suggested that students who attended private schools for their entire school career achieved at higher levels than did students who transferred from a public school into a private school participating in the PAVE program. Further, the evaluation suggested that the longer transfer students stayed in participating private schools, the greater their achievement.

Unfortunately, since the data gathered depended entirely on the voluntary cooperation of parents, the findings are suspect and no conclusion can be drawn from the evaluation's results.

Indianapolis. The Educational Choice Charitable Trust was established in 1991 with a $1.2 million grant from J. Patrick Rooney, chairman and CEO of the Golden Rule Insurance Company. The trust provides education vouchers worth half the cost of private school tuition up to a maximum of $800. Families with children who qualify for the free or reduced-price lunch program and live in the Indianapolis school district are eligible. Half the money in the program was reserved for families whose children were in private schools prior to the creation of the program.

In March 1996 the Hudson Institute issued a report by David Weinschrott and Sally Kilgore assessing the impact of the program.[52] Public school students, but not voucher students, showed a drop-off in reading, language, and math scores in sixth and eighth grade.

Weinschrott and Kilgore described their evaluation framework as "informal." It was based on a small number of voucher students enrolled in a handful of voucher schools. The analysis did not control for differences in student characteristics, test scores prior to the voucher program, or other potentially significant variables that may have influenced the findings.

New York. The New York City School Choice Scholarships Foundation (SCSF) was established in 1997 with $5 million of its $7 million commitment coming from New York businesspeople. SCSF offers tuition vouchers worth up to $1,400 to students whose family income makes them eligible for the school free-lunch program. Eighty-five percent of the scholarships are reserved for public school students whose test scores are below the citywide median. In its first year (1997-98) the program offered scholarships for up to 1,300 students and actually placed about 1,200 students in private schools. In 1998-99, an additional 1,000 students participated in the program. SCSF has made four-year commitments to the current participants and will add more students as funding permits.

Of parents expressing interest in the program, a randomly selected group were interviewed to determine their eligibility, while their children (except for kindergartners) were administered the Iowa Test of Basic Skills in reading and math. A lottery determined which eligible students would be offered vouchers.

In the spring of 1997, Mathematica Policy Research and Paul Peterson of the Harvard Program on Education Policy and Governance began a three-year evaluation of the performance of students entering the New York SCSF Program in 1997-98.[53] The evaluation examines two issues. First, it compares the achievement of about 750 students who used vouchers with that of 960 students whose families sought but did not receive a scholarship. (Ten percent of the nonvoucher students ultimately attended private school anyway.) Second, the evaluation also compares the achievement of 1,000 students offered a voucher, including some students that did not use one, with that of the same control group of 960 students.

23

A limitation of the first comparison is that, though a random group of students received scholarship offers, a *nonrandom* group appeared to have accepted offers. According to Peterson, Myers, and Howell, families that used scholarships had higher incomes and more education than did families that did not use scholarships.[54] Peterson, Myers, and Howell used standard statistical procedures to control for differences between voucher users and students not offered a scholarship. However, they did not provide enough information about these procedures to permit a complete evaluation of them.

The second comparison gets around the nonrandom nature of the group that actually used the scholarships by taking advantage of the "natural experiment" resulting from the use of a random lottery to select those offered vouchers. As a result of this lottery, the background characteristics of those offered scholarships and of those not offered scholarships may be assumed to be, on average, the same. Any differences between the two groups can be attributed to the "offer" of a scholarship. However, this comparison is somewhat difficult to interpret. Why would the offer of a scholarship be expected to make a difference to the performance of students who do not actually accept the scholarship?

In November 1998 Peterson, Myers, and Howell released first-year evaluation results. They found that being offered a voucher raised performance significantly in math in second, third, and fifth grades and in reading in fifth grade. In third grade, being offered a voucher was negatively correlated with math and reading achievement but not significantly so. The effect on achievement of actually receiving a voucher was statistically significant in math in second, fourth, and fifth grade and in reading in fifth grade. In third grade, receiving a voucher was negatively correlated with math and reading achievement but not significantly so.

Peterson, Myers, and Howell increased the number of so-called significant results by using a statistical method that requires assuming that vouchers can increase but not decrease student achievement.[55] The conflicting results reported in the literature on vouchers and public versus private schools make this assumption

24

questionable. Without this assumption, only the results for fourth-grade math, fifth-grade reading, and combined fourth- and fifth-grade math are significant. In addition, the differences between the results across grade levels are hard to interpret. This suggests that the results should be treated with caution until more data are available.

Since the Peterson, Myers, and Howell evaluation of the New York SCSF program constructs comparison groups, it is more informative than the Peterson, Greene, and Howell analysis of the two Hope Schools in Cleveland. However, as Peterson, Myers, and Howell acknowledge, their SCSF evaluation involved a small number of students and the effect of a much larger program could have quite different program outcomes. A number of characteristics of the schools attended by voucher students in the New York experiment might not exist in a large-scale experiment. For example, compared to the schools attended by the control group, the voucher schools had small classes and were somewhat more racially integrated. Parents perceived that voucher schools had fewer problems with safety, fighting, cheating, missing classes, being late for school, and destroying property.

The frailty of positive findings from participation in voucher programs is suggested by the ad hoc and inconsistent ways that Peterson and co-authors explain findings from New York and from Milwaukee. In their analysis of the Milwaukee Parental Choice Program, Greene, Peterson, and Du find significant achievement effects only for students who had been in the program for three or four years.[56] They hypothesize that participation in a voucher program has a cumulative effect, with positive results appearing only in the third and fourth years, after students have been socialized in their new setting. In discussing the New York program, Peterson, Myers, and Howell hypothesize that they found significant results only for fourth- and fifth-grade students because vouchers are a more potent intervention for older students. They add that smaller classes may be more potent for younger students — an explanation at odds with the fact that students at voucher schools in the New York program attended smaller classes than did students in the control group.

In discussing their first-year New York results, Peterson, Myers, and Howell argue that the magnitudes of the positive achievement effects observed "do not differ materially from those observed in" the Tennessee class-size reduction program.[57] This comparison is problematic because of the instability of most of the SCSF findings compared with the Tennessee results. Charles Achilles, one of the Tennessee experiment principal investigators, pointed out that since the students in the SCSF evaluation are about 95% minority, it might be more appropriate to compare SCSF effect sizes with the effect sizes observed for Tennessee minority students.[58] When this comparison is made, the Tennessee effect sizes (between 0.30 and 0.40) are much larger and much more stable than the effect sizes reported by Peterson, Myers, and Howell (-0.09 to 0.27).

Washington, D.C. The Washington Scholarship Fund (WSF) was established in 1993 to provide vouchers to low-income students. Its funding comes from a variety of individuals, including John Walton and Ted Forstmann, and foundations, such as the Lynde and Harry Bradley Foundation. In the fall of 1997, 460 WSF participants were attending 72 private schools. Beginning with the 1998-99 school year, the program planned to offer vouchers worth up to $2,200 to more than 1,000 students in grades K-8. No family with an income higher than 2.5 times the poverty level may participate. Families with incomes that fall below the poverty line are eligible for vouchers worth up to 60% of the cost of private school tuition.

Dayton, Ohio. For the 1998-99 school year, the Parents Advancing Choice in Education (PACE) program in Dayton, Ohio, offered vouchers to 530 students previously enrolled in public schools and 250 students previously enrolled in private schools. The program pays up to 60% of the tuition at one of 20 private schools participating in the program, up to a maximum of $1,200. The program is funded by the Thomas B. Fordham Foundation and a consortium of Dayton community leaders.

The WSF and PACE programs are being evaluated by the Harvard Program on Education Policy and Governance, the Northern

Illinois University Social Science Research Unit, and (for the PACE program only) the University of Dayton.[59] In each program, a randomized design similar to that used to evaluate the New York School Choice Scholarship program is being implemented. At this point, no achievement data are available for either program.

San Antonio. San Antonio has two private voucher programs, both of which are funded by the CEO America Foundation. The first began in 1992 and offers a voucher worth up to half the cost of tuition (to a maximum of $800) to any K-8 student eligible for free or reduced-price lunches who resides in Bexar County, Texas. Students may attend public or private schools. Godwin, Kemerer, and Martinez compared the effects of public school choice and private voucher programs in San Antonio.[60] The small number of students (85) for whom baseline (1991-92) and final-year (1995-96) test score data were available and the limited nature of the results make their achievement findings of little value.

In April 1998 the CEO America Foundation and James Leininger committed $50 million over a period of 10 years to launch the Horizon Program. It is the first private voucher program in the country to offer a voucher to every low-income student within a single school district (the Edgewood Independent School District in San Antonio, Texas). Any K-12 student who is eligible for a free or reduced-price lunch and who resides in the district may participate. Vouchers may pay up to 100% of a participating school's tuition, to a maximum of $3,600 (grades K-8) for schools in the district and a maximum of $2,000 (grades K-8) for schools outside the district. For grades 9-12 the program pays up to $4,000 for schools in the district and up to $3,500 for schools outside the district.[61]

The evaluation of the Horizon Program is being conducted by David Myers (Mathematica Policy Research), Paul Peterson (Harvard University), Jay Greene (University of Texas), and Rodolfo de la Garza (Thomas Rivera Policy Institute). The first report, issued in Spetember 1999, provided preliminary information about the children who attended private schools through the Horizon Program and about their parents.

While no strong evidence exists that voucher programs improve student achievement, all parties to the voucher debate at least agree that improving achievement is a desirable goal. But achievement is not the only issue in the debate. People favor or oppose vouchers in part because they hold different social and political values. Professor Peter Cookson (Teachers College, Columbia University) calls the battle over school choice a struggle over the "soul" of American public education. Jeffrey Henig sees in the struggle a conflict over the type of society Americans want to call into being.[62]

Indeed, vouchers could increase inequity by diverting money from students currently served by the public schools to students who already go to private schools. For example, rather than providing Milwaukee Public School children with choice, the expansion of the Milwaukee voucher and charter school programs appears to be diverting money from children in the public schools and subsidizing families who were already sending their children to private schools. According to Henry Levin (Stanford University), the 5,902 students enrolled in either charter or voucher schools cost the Milwaukee Public Schools $29,214,900 in revenue in 1997-98. Of the 5,902 voucher and charter school students, only 1,379 had attended the Milwaukee Public Schools the previous year.[63]

Levin estimated that a national voucher program that included all current private school students and that offered the full range of services provided by public schools would cost $33 billion annually. The costs of accommodating additional students in private schools, record-keeping and monitoring, and providing transportation would add another $40 billion, bringing the total to $73 billion, about 25% of the current cost of public education nationally.

Private schools may have considerable symbolic value for their students, parents, and alumni, but rarely for others. By increasing the number and enrollment of private schools, while decreasing those of public schools, large-scale voucher programs would diminish the symbolic value of public schools. In so doing, they could reinforce social fragmentation of the American community along ethnic and racial lines. This possibility is hinted at by the fact that most Hispanics in Milwaukee went to just one Choice school.

Large-scale voucher programs also may have the potential to increase inequality and the stratification of students by family income as well as social background. This concern is supported both by theoretical arguments and by empirical evidence on large-scale school choice programs. Programs the size of the ones in Milwaukee and Cleveland are too small to have much effect on inequality.

There is evidence that school choice programs, including public school choice as well as voucher and charter school programs, increase student stratification by income and other family background characteristics but do not necessarily produce academic gains.

Evidence from Arizona corroborates the fear that a large-scale school choice program may increase stratification in the schools based on income, race, and ethnicity. Casey D. Cobb and Gene V. Glass found that Arizona charter schools are increasing racial segregation in public education. Minority students are disproportionately enrolled in charter schools with non-college-preparatory curricula.[64] Large-scale voucher programs would share many of the characteristics of Arizona's largely unregulated charter school program and may, therefore, similarly reduce education equity.

A 1999 Michigan State University study finds that Michigan's choice programs, including charter schools and inter-district transfer arrangements, have resulted in "creaming," not of the most academically talented students, but of those least expensive to educate. Charter schools frequently offer only elementary grade levels, avoiding the more costly secondary grades that require more sophisticated science laboratories and libraries, athletic equipment, and teachers with specialized degrees. In addition, the study finds, three-quarters of Michigan's charter schools did not offer any special education services, and those that did provided less extensive and less costly services than public schools in their area. As for inter-district transfer agreements, the Michigan State

University researchers find that, though half of the state's school districts now accept students from other districts, many of the wealthiest districts do not. The lack of participation of the most affluent districts means that students do not have equal access to the state's best-funded public schools.[65]

Godwin, Kemerer, and Martinez, in their analyses of the characteristics of families that chose to participate in either public or private school choice programs in San Antonio, find significant differences between choosing and non-choosing families. Choosing families had more education, higher incomes, higher employment levels, and fewer children and were less likely to be on welfare, less likely to be African American, and more likely to be two-parent families. Choosing families also had higher educational expectations and were more active in their children's education. In addition, their children had higher standardized test scores.[66]

A 1992 Carnegie Foundation report evaluated choice programs around the country and reaches the following conclusions: 1) To the extent that choice programs benefit children at all, they benefit the children of better educated parents. 2) Choice programs require additional money to operate. 3) Choice programs have the potential to widen the gap between rich and poor school districts. 4) School choice does not necessarily improve student achievement.[67] Bruce Fuller, in a 1995 review, drew conclusions similar to those of the Carnegie report.[68]

In a review of the research on school choice in three countries (the United States, Great Britain, and New Zealand), Geoff Whitty finds little evidence to support the contention that the creation of education "markets" increases student achievement. However, he does find that education "markets" make existing inequalities in the provision of education worse. Martin Carnoy draws a similar conclusion based on an analysis of the effects of school privatization in Chile and other countries.[69]

Of course, the current public school system stratifies students by family income and education background. One of the most important means by which this stratification occurs is residential choice. The more affluent, educated, and committed to education seek to live where their children can attend good schools. The children of the poor are then often left behind to struggle in substandard, underfunded schools. In his 1995 book, *Private Vouchers,* Terry Moe, one of the most prominent voucher advocates, argues that vouchers are a force for greater education equity because they provide poor students with a choice of schools.[70] In a voucher system, however, families would sort themselves among schools on the basis of income, education preferences, and knowledge about schooling. Under the current system, families who send their children to public schools sort themselves among residential locations (and, therefore, school districts) on the basis not only of these factors, but also others, such as the cost and quality of housing, distance to work, and availability of recreational opportunities. For this reason, private schools under a large-scale voucher program are likely to be more internally homogeneous (with respect to students' socioeconomic background) than are public schools under the current system. With public schools, some of the poor get a chance to attend the same schools as their middle- and upper-income peers. With large-scale voucher programs, fewer of the poor are likely to have this opportunity. Vouchers would then be a force for education inequity.

Although not inherent in voucher systems, there are additional features of most voucher proposals that would worsen education inequity. Most voucher proposals propose considerably lower levels of funding than would result from giving students a per capita share of current spending on education. With this funding, children of affluent parents already in private schools could still spend more than they do currently on education. Children of poor parents would have an even smaller amount to spend on their education. Second, most proposals, including the Milwaukee program, in effect allow private schools to exclude some special needs students, because the schools need not provide services on which those students depend. Some proposals, unlike Milwaukee, would allow schools complete authority over whom to admit and

31

whom to exclude. Terry Moe acknowledges the danger that this poses. He argues that it can be addressed through careful attention to the design of voucher programs.[71]

It is instructive that the political figure most closely identified with the contemporary voucher movement, Wisconsin state legislator Polly Williams, now expresses concerns about the political pressure to create voucher programs that would increase education inequity. She told the *Boston Globe* in October 1998:

> I knew from the beginning that white Republicans and rich, right-wing foundations that praised me and used me to validate their agenda would do it only so long as it suited their needs. . . . This is why most black groups like the NAACP are against vouchers because without the income cap, choice just becomes a free-market program that keeps richer families happy and Catholic and Lutheran schools solvent with state money without any commitment to improve public schools. . . . Too many people in the voucher crowd exploit low-income black children, saying we are creating vouchers for them when what they really have in mind is bringing in a Trojan horse. . . . I've never seen a situation where low-income people, when they have to compete in education with people with far more resources, come out equal.[72]

Taken together, the evidence from the Milwaukee and Cleveland voucher programs, as well as private voucher programs, suggests that education vouchers have an uncertain upside as a large-scale reform. If voucher programs increase education inequality, they have a potentially large downside.

SMALLER CLASSES

The effect of class size on achievement has been studied for more than a century. Glen Robinson and James Wittebols of the Educational Research Service trace the beginning of research on class size to the work of J.M. Rice in 1893.[73] In a 1902 study, Rice concluded that there was no relationship between class size and student achievement.[74] In subsequent decades, the heyday of the industrial model of schooling, much research on class size aimed at ascertaining how large classes could be made without significant reductions in student learning.

Howard Blake's 1954 review of 267 different studies marks the beginning of modern class-size research. Of the 85 original studies Blake found that focused on elementary and secondary education, 22 met his criteria for qualifying as scientific studies. Of these 22, 16 found that children learned more in smaller classes, three favored larger classes, and three were inconclusive.[75]

During the 1960s and 1970s, attention turned to the effect that small-group instruction might have on children from low-income families.[76] Many studies in this period statistically explored whether Chapter 1 funding improved the performance of low-income students relative to comparable or more advantaged ones who received no support. This research left unanswered the question of whether low-income children benefit from smaller classes.

Recent Class-Size Research

The current interest in class-size research can be traced to an influential and controversial 1978 meta-analysis of class-size studies from more than a dozen countries by Professor Gene Glass of Arizona State University and Mary Lee Smith, currently director of the Division of Educational Leadership and Policy Studies at Arizona State University.[77] Glass and Smith conclude that small classes produce higher levels of student achievement than large classes do. For example, they find that being taught in a one-on-one tutorial as opposed to a 40-student class improved student performance by 30 percentile ranks. Glass and Smith argue that, to be most effective, classes should have about 15 students.

Robinson and Wittebols criticize the Glass and Smith study for drawing conclusions from too few studies and relying too heavily on research on individual tutoring.[78] Professor Robert Slavin of Johns Hopkins University also considers Glass and Smith's analysis flawed because it does not adequately take into account qualitative distinctions between studies.[79] In Slavin's view, except for studies of class sizes of one, Glass and Smith's evidence that class-size reductions raise achievement is weak.

Indiana. Against this backdrop of controversy over the relationship between class size and student achievement, Indiana launched Project Prime Time, a statewide class-size reduction effort.[80] In 1984, Indiana school corporations (the Indiana equivalent of school districts) became eligible to receive state funds to pay the salaries of additional teachers and teacher aides that are necessary to reduce first-grade class-size averages to 18, or to 24 if a teacher aide was in the room. In 1985 the state extended this arrangement to second grade, and in 1986 corporations gained the option of adding either kindergarten or third grade. Now in its 15th year, Prime Time today subsidizes the salaries needed to move toward average class targets of 18 students per teacher in K-1 and 20 in grades two and three. In recent years, Prime Time has been accompanied by an extensive effort to provide professional development and to disseminate instructional methods that take full advantage of small class sizes.

Research on Prime Time shows mixed results. In 1990, David Gilman and Christopher Tillitski, after reviewing four studies, concluded that Prime Time class-size reductions had produced no achievement advantage.[81] They caution that their findings do not necessarily imply that any class-size reduction program will fail. Prime Time was, in their judgment, a poorly conceived, hastily implemented program with inadequate provision for training teachers and for systematic evaluation.

State-funded evaluations of Prime Time, conducted in 1987 and 1992, show positive but not definitive results.[82] The 1992 evaluation examined the experiences and test scores of 21 schools in 12 districts but did not include a control group.[83] The evaluation found that, after two consecutive years in Prime Time, third-grade students outscored the statewide average student on the Indiana State Test of Educational Progress (ISTEP), a battery of language, math, and reading tests.[84] Students in small classes in grades one and two beat the statewide average by more than did students in small classes in grades two and three. Sixth-graders who had Prime Time in first and second grade did better on the ISTEP than the statewide average, but sixth-graders who had Prime Time in grades two and three did not, possibly because they were drawn mostly from large city and poor rural districts.[85]

Tennessee. Tennessee launched the STAR program in the mid-1980s. Key Tennessee legislators knew of the Indiana Prime Time program and a class-size study conducted in Nashville.[86] They were particularly influenced by Glass and Smith's meta-analysis, which suggested reducing class size to about 15. Mindful of the cost of reducing class size, the legislature wanted to study the impact of reducing class size in the early grades before adopting a class-size reduction policy.

In 1985, the Tennessee legislature passed, and Governor Lamar Alexander signed into law, funding for a statewide class-size experiment. The STAR study followed a group of students from kindergarten through third grade. Since Tennessee did not require kindergarten, many STAR students entered the study as first-graders. The STAR study began in the fall of 1985 in 79 schools within 42 school districts throughout the state.

Researchers classified schools as: 1) inner-city (metropolitan-area schools in which more than half the students received free or reduced-price lunches), 2) urban, 3) suburban, and 4) rural.

Within each participating school, the state Department of Education randomly assigned teachers and students to one of three types of classes: small (S) classes (typically 13-17 students), regular (R) classes (typically 22-25 students), and regular classes with a full-time instructional aide (RA) (typically 22-25 students).

With one important exception, once assigned to a class type, students stayed in that type of class as long as they remained in STAR. The major exception was that students in R and RA classes during kindergarten were randomly reassigned to either R or RA classes for first grade. (The researchers observed no significant differences between R and RA student performance in kindergarten.) While it complicates analysis of the STAR experiment, the reassignment does not interfere with the central findings regarding the performance of students in small classes versus the other two types.

To ensure that curriculum differences, leadership style, school climate, and other school-specific factors did not influence the results, all schools participating in the project had to be large enough to have all three types of classes at all four grade levels. The STAR project also required that there be no changes in participating schools other than the establishment of the three types of classes.

STAR is one of the few truly scientific experiments ever conducted in education. It is also a large study that involved about 6,500 students each year. In all, 11,600 different students participated in Project STAR, of whom 1,842 remained in the same type of class for all four years and 2,571 remained in the same type of class for grades 1-3.

Students in STAR were tested in reading and math on the Stanford Achievement Test and the Tennessee Basic Skills First test. STAR researchers compared improvements in achievement each year by each class type. They also compared the performance of students in small classes for three consecutive years with the performance of students in each type of regular class for three consecutive years.

STAR researchers found that students in small classes outperformed students in both R and RA classes across the board in all geographic areas and at all grade levels. Regular classrooms with a teacher's aide showed a slight but not statistically significant achievement advantage over regular classrooms in first grade. Jayne Boyd-Zaharias and Helen Pate-Bain reported in 1998 that their analysis of STAR data found no achievement advantage for classes of 25 students with a full-time teacher's aide compared to classes of 25 without an aide. This was true in grades K-3 and in a follow-up study of students in grades 4-8.[87]

Averaged over four years, students in small classes had an advantage of a bit more than eight percentile ranks over students in regular classes in reading and a bit less than eight percentile ranks in math. The effect size in reading averaged over four years was about 0.26. In math it was 0.23.[88]

In a May 1997 reexamination of the STAR data, economist Alan Krueger of Princeton University confirmed the original findings of the STAR investigators. Krueger controlled for other measured factors that might influence performance, including student characteristics (race, gender, eligibility for free lunch, whether the student was new to the school, etc.) and teacher characteristics (race, gender, experience, and education qualifications). Because students and teachers were initially placed at random into the three types of classes, these characteristics would not be expected to influence the effect of class size on performance. As anticipated, Krueger found that controlling for these variables has very little effect. He still found overall effect sizes that range from 0.19 to 0.28 in each of the four years, similar to the range reported in the original STAR analysis.[89]

The original STAR results may be understated because some classes labeled as small were actually larger than some labeled as large. (Since the number of students in a grade does not fall into multiples of 13-17 and 22-25, it is unavoidable that small and regular classes be distributed around these targets.) A research team headed by Professor Barbara Nye and B. DeWayne Fulton (Tennessee State University) re-estimated the performance difference of small classes and regular classes after removing all small classes that did not have 12-14 students and all regular classes that did not have at least 23 students from the sample. They reported effect-size advantages for small classes that average 0.56 for reading and 0.47 for math.[90]

The STAR study also found that small classes especially raised achievement in inner-city Tennessee classrooms with large concentrations of minority students.[91] Jeremy Finn and Charles Achilles conclude in a recent review paper that "in most comparisons, the benefit to minority students is about *two to three times as large as that for whites.*"[92] Krueger also finds that lower-achieving, minority, and poor students benefit the most from attending smaller classes.[93]

Charles Achilles, Jeremy Finn, and Helen Bain reported that when both white and nonwhite Tennessee students began kindergarten in small classes, 87% of white and 86% of nonwhite first-graders passed the Basic Skills First reading test. For students who began kindergarten in regular classes, the nonwhite first-grade pass rate trailed the white pass rate by 12 percentage points.[94]

In a review of the research literature on the white-black test gap and on class size, including the Tennessee experience, Steven Bingham concluded that small class size in the early grades is an effective achievement gap-reduction strategy. He maintained that minority children should be placed in small classes early (preferably in kindergarten) and remain in a small class for at least two years.[95]

The STAR study found that small classes increased promotion rates from each grade. Over the four years of the study, 80.2% of students in small classes moved up to the next grade the following year, compared with 72.6% of students in regular classes. Raising promotion rates for each grade saves money by reducing the number of students taught twice at each grade level.[96]

In addition, when more students are held back, the R and RA classes at the next grade level end up with fewer low-scoring students. If students in R and RA classes had been promoted at the same rate as those in small classes, the relative test scores of R and RA classes might have been even lower. The higher retention-in-grade rates of R and RA classes may cause the estimate of the additional benefit of several years in a small class to be understated.

Finally, the Tennessee experiment provides some evidence that small classes mitigate the negative effect of large schools documented by William Fowler and Herbert Walberg (University of Illinois at Chicago).[97] According to Achilles, students in regular classes achieved less well in large schools than in small schools. Students in small classes did as well or nearly as well in large schools as in small schools.[98]

Because of the STAR study's size and careful design, Harvard Professor Frederick Mosteller, in a report to the American Academy of Arts and Sciences, characterized the study as "one of the great experiments in education in United States history."[99] Nevertheless, debate about the policy implications of the STAR results continues.

Are the Benefits of Smaller Classes Cumulative?
Do the Benefits Last?

Recent debate about the Tennessee STAR experiment centers on two questions that turn out to be related. 1) Are the benefits of smaller classes cumulative? 2) Do the benefits last?

Initial research on the STAR experiment indicated that most of the gain appeared the first year children attended a smaller class, with the achievement gap between small and regular classes holding steady but not increasing in subsequent years. Based on this understanding, Eric Hanushek argued in a February 1998 paper that the Tennessee results support, at most, movement toward small kindergarten and first-grade classes.[100]

Contrary to Hanushek's conclusion, an increasing body of research indicates that achievement benefits do increase with additional years in small classes. Krueger found that while the achievement of students in small classes jumped by about four percentile ranks in the first year a student attended a small class, it improved by almost an additional percentile rank for each additional year. The initial effect was highly significant and the incremental improvement in subsequent years was on the margin of statistical significance.[101]

Additional new research on STAR students relies on a database constructed for the Lasting Benefits Study (LBS), an analysis of the achievement of small- and regular-class STAR students in higher grades. A STAR student is defined in the LBS as any student who spent at least third grade in a STAR classroom.[102]

Through eighth grade, the original LBS studies found that students in small classes during part or all of K-3 continued to outperform graduates of R and RA classes by statistically significant amounts.[103] The achievement advantage for minority students who participated in small classes remained larger than that for white students.[104] Lasting benefits from small K-3 classes were found in a wide spectrum of subjects, including reading, language, math, study skills, science, and social studies.[105]

The Lasting Benefits Study showed eighth-grade effect sizes of 0.04 to 0.08,[106] seventh-grade effect sizes that ranged from 0.08 to 0.16,[107] sixth-grade effect sizes of 0.14 to 0.26,[108] fifth-grade results ranging from 0.17 to 0.34,[109] and fourth-grade effect sizes of 0.11 to 0.16.[110] STAR students from small classes continue to outperform students in regular classes; but the presence of a teacher's aide continues to have very little, if any, impact on achievement.

The new research using the LBS database separately examined children who attended small classes for one, two, three, or four years. Barbara Nye, Larry V. Hedges, and Spyros Konstantopoulos found that statistically significant benefits from small classes persisted to eighth grade only for students who spent at least two grades in a small class. On eighth-grade math, reading, and science tests, the effect size for students who attended small classes for four years was 0.3 to 0.37, similar to the effect size for these students in grades four and six. By eighth grade, the achievement benefit of spending four years in small classes equaled four or more times that of spending one year in a small class, 80% more than that of spending two years in small classes, and 20% to 30% more than that of spending three years in small classes. In other words, the incremental benefit of each additional year in small classes appears to be roughly the same.[111]

David Grissmer of RAND pointed out that Nye, Hedges, and Konstantopoulos' findings imply a bigger benefit from the third and fourth years of small classes than Krueger's estimates (described above).[112] Grissmer hypothesized that this may partly reflect differences between the samples. Since Nye, Hedges, and Konstantopoulos used the Lasting Benefits Study (LBS) database, all the students in their sample took the third-grade test. Many of the students in their sample with one and two years in small classes entered small classes in second and third grade. In the full STAR sample that Krueger used, a high proportion of the students in small classes for one and two years entered and reported test scores in kindergarten and first grade. In different ways, then, both sets of results underscore the value of small classes in kindergarten and first grade. They also point to the benefits of additional years in small classes, with Nye, Hedges, and Konstantopoulos' results raising questions about the durability of the "jump" in achievement after one year if it is not consolidated by additional years in small classes.

Finn and Achilles added another dimension to the literature on the lasting benefits of small classes by converting the achievement difference between small and regular class students into "grade equivalents."[113] The effect sizes normally used to measure the achievement benefit of small classes divide the average test score difference in a grade by the variability (or standard deviation) of that test score. However, student performance varies more in higher grades, increasing the denominator in effect-size measurements.

Grade equivalents (GEs) offer another way of looking at the effect of smaller classes. The grade equivalent of a test score is the grade level for which that score was the median score.[114] For example, if the median test score of students with four months of fourth grade was 100, the grade-equivalent of a score of 100 would be third grade plus four months. Using grade equivalents, a difference in average test scores between small and regular classes can be converted into a difference measured in grade-equivalent months of schooling. Table 3 converts the benefits from small K-3 classes into GE months of schooling. Table 4 does the same for the benefits of attending four years in small classes.

Based on their GE analysis, Finn and Achilles concluded that the achievement effect of being in a small class continues and generally increases from grade to grade.[115]

In September 1997, Health and Education Research Operative Services (HEROS) published a study of the extent to which 10th-grade students who had been enrolled in STAR small K-3 classes retained an achievement advantage over students who had been in regular classes and regular classes with a teacher's aide.[116] The study analyzed the relative performance of these students on the Tennessee Competency Test. It found that the performance of students who had attended small classes was not significantly better than that of students who had been in regular classes. However, the researchers did find that significantly more of the former small-class students than regular-class students had passed the test by eighth grade.

STAR students who graduated on schedule would have completed high school in spring 1998. In April 1999, Alan Krueger and Diane Whitmore reported preliminary results of an analysis of the rate at which a sample of 9,397 STAR study participants took college-entrance exams (the ACT and SAT tests) as seniors.[117] Overall, 43.7% of students assigned to a small class in their first Project STAR year took the ACT or SAT exam, compared to 40% of students in regular classes and 39.9% of students in regular classes with an aide. These differences between S-class students and R- and RA-class students were statistically significant at the 0.05 level.

Attending small classes raised the proportion of black students who took a college entrance exam by substantially more; 40.2% of black students in small classes took either the ACT or SAT, compared to 31.7% of students in regular classes. Attending a small class reduced the black-white gap in college-entrance test-taking by 54%.

Students initially assigned to a class with 21-25 students were more likely to take the ACT or SAT exam than were students assigned to classes with 26-30 students. They were less likely to take one of the exams than students initially assigned to classes with 16-20 students.

Even though significantly higher proportions of small-class students took the college-entrance exams, their average scores were virtually the same as those of students in regular-size classes. The same held true for the subgroups examined.

Preliminary findings from another ongoing study, based on the high school experiences of more than 3,000 former STAR participants, showed that 72% of small-class participants graduated from high school on schedule compared to 66% of regular-class students and 65% of students from regular classes with a teacher's aide. While 23% of regular-class students and 26% of regular-class-with-aide students dropped out, only 19% of small-class students dropped out.[118]

Table 3. The Tennessee small-class advantage measured in grade equivalent months of schooling.

	Kindergarten	Grade 1	Grade 2	Grade 3
Mathematics	1.6 months	2.8 months	3.3 months	2.8 months
Reading	0.5 months	1.2 months	3.9 months	4.6 months
Word Study Skills	0.5 months	0.8 months	4.7 months	4.7 months

Source: Jeremy D. Finn, Susan B. Gerber, Charles M. Achilles, and Jayne Boyd-Zaharias, "Short- and Long-Term Effects of Small Classes" (paper prepared for the conference on the Economics of School Reform, Hebrew University, Jerusalem, 23-26 May 1999), available from finn@acsu.buffalo.edu.

Table 4. The achievement benefits in grades 4, 6, and 8 of having spent four years in small K-3 classes, measured in grade equivalent months of schooling.

	Grade 4	Grade 6	Grade 8
Mathematics	5.9 months	8.4 months	1 year, 1 month
Reading	9.1 months	9.2 months	1 year, 2 months
Science	7.6 months	6.7 months	1 year, 1 month

Source: Jeremy D. Finn, Susan B. Gerber, Charles M. Achilles, and Jayne Boyd-Zaharias, "Short- and Long-Term Effects of Small Classes" (paper prepared for the conference on the Economics of School Reform, Hebrew University, Jerusalem, 23-26 May 1999), available from finn@acsu.buffalo.edu.

Future research on the STAR students by HEROS will focus on experience in higher education and on such social outcomes as juvenile detention, adult imprisonment, welfare, and employment experience.

Project Challenge

Beginning in 1989 Tennessee followed up its STAR experiment by establishing Project Challenge, which provided the money necessary to reduce K-3 class size in 16 of the state's poorest school districts. These districts typically placed low on achievement rankings of Tennessee's 138 school districts. After the implementation of Project Challenge, student achievement in math and reading improved both in comparison to the performance of previous students in these districts and in relation to other schools in the state.[119] Between 1989-90 and 1993-94, Project Challenge school districts' average ranking on grade-two test results improved from 97th-highest to 78th-highest in reading and from 90th-highest to 56th-highest in math. Therefore, student achievement in these poor districts in 1993-94 was only a little below that of the median district in the state in reading and above the median in math.

Nevada Class Size Reduction Act

Nevada passed its Class Size Reduction Act in 1989 and implemented it in first grade and selected kindergartens in the 1990-91 school year. Second grade was added to the program in 1991-92, and some third-grade classrooms were included in 1996-97.[120] Only 60% to 70% of the first- and second-grade classrooms in the Nevada program reduce class size by establishing a classroom with one teacher and 15 students. The rest use flexible groupings, multi-age groupings, two teachers sharing a classroom, and other strategies.

According to Mary Snow of the Nevada Department of Education, Nevada has never devoted the resources necessary for a full-scale, systematic evaluation of its class-size reduction ini-

44

Key Findings from Analyses of the
Tennessee STAR Experiment

1. On every achievement measure in every year through eighth grade, there were statistically significant differences between the performance of students in small classes and those in the two types of regular classes.
2. Every type of district — inner-city, urban, suburban, and rural — enjoyed significant gains from small classes.
3. In each grade, minorities and students attending inner-city schools enjoyed greater small-class advantages than did whites on some or all measures.
4. The same benefits from small classes were found for boys and girls alike.
5. Rural small classes achieved the highest test scores.
6. For students who spent all four years (K-3) in small classes, the average achievement advantage on math, reading, and science tests grows from 6-9 months of schooling in grade four to more than one year of schooling in grade eight.
7. Students who attended small classes took college-entrance exams at significantly higher rates than did students who attended the two types of regular classes.
8. Students who attended small classes graduated from high school on schedule at significantly higher rates than did students who attended the two types of regular classes.

tiative.[121] Snow published evaluations of the program in 1993, 1997, 1998, and 1999 and expects to publish a school-level evaluation in 2000. James Pollard and Kim Yap of the Northwest Regional Educational Laboratory prepared an evaluation in 1995.

Snow's 1999 evaluation examined the test scores of fourth- and eighth-grade students in reading, language, and math. For both grade levels, there were small but statistically significant improvements in overall test scores for all three subjects. However, when Snow analyzed scores by subgroup (ethnicity, English proficiency, special education, and socioeconomic status), she noted that the association between smaller class size and higher test scores was consistent only among white, Hispanic, and Asian-American students in fourth grade and among white and Asian-American students in eighth grade.[122]

In the 1998 evaluation, Snow reported that the mean scores of students who were in small classes for two years (grades one and two) were slightly higher than for students who were not in small classes. The differences were statistically significant overall. Smaller classes were not significantly related to higher test scores for limited-English-proficiency students or for students of low socioeconomic status. However, smaller classes were associated with higher test scores for exceptional education students.[123]

Snow's 1997 evaluation shows that having attended small classes in earlier grades significantly improves mean test scores in language, math, and reading for fourth-graders. Improvements in scores generally were small, especially for reading.[124] However, Pollard and Yap's 1995 evaluation found that, in parts of the state, students in larger classes scored better in reading than those in smaller classes did.[125]

The mean scores for students with lower socioeconomic status and for minority students do not show differences based on participation in the Nevada Class Size Reduction Program. Also, results from Nevada generally favor teaching in self-contained classes as opposed to team teaching in rooms of about 30 students.

In a 1995 opinion survey, 61% of Nevada parents believed that the benefits warranted paying the estimated $852 per student for smaller classes. Less than 10% of the parents believed that the benefits were not worth the cost.[126]

Wisconsin: Student Achievement Guarantee in Education

Wisconsin implemented its statewide Student Achievement Guarantee in Education (SAGE) program in 1996-97. SAGE seeks to increase the academic achievement of children living in poverty by reducing the student-teacher ratio in kindergarten through third grade to 15:1.[127] Participation in SAGE requires a school to implement a rigorous academic curriculum, provide before- and after-school activities for students and community members, and implement professional development and accountability plans.

All districts with a school that enrolls 50% or more low-income children participated. Within these districts, any school enrolling 30% or more low-income children could apply. Each eligible district except Milwaukee could designate one school as a SAGE school. Milwaukee was allowed 10 SAGE schools.

Schools entering the program had to agree to remain in SAGE for its five-year duration. They also had to submit an annual "Achievement Guarantee Contract" to the state Department of Public Instruction. This contract explains how the school plans to implement the SAGE program requirements. Schools are allowed wide latitude in developing their plans. Upon accepting a school into SAGE, the state provides up to an additional $2,000 per low-income student enrolled in SAGE classrooms. The original legislation specified that no new schools would be admitted after the start of the 1996-97 school year. However, SAGE proved so popular that the state legislature agreed to expand it in 1997 and again in 1999.

SAGE is designed to be implemented in stages. Kindergarten and first-grade classes entered the program in 1996-97, second grade was added in 1997-98, and third grade in 1998-99. All classrooms at the appropriate grade level in participating schools must have a student-teacher ratio of no more than 15:1. During the 1996-97 school year, SAGE was implemented in 30 schools in 21 school districts throughout Wisconsin.

The legislation creating SAGE requires an annual evaluation of the program and a fifth-year final report on the effect of the program on academic achievement. Professor Alex Molnar and co-researchers at the School of Education, University of Wisconsin-Milwaukee are conducting this legislatively mandated evaluation.[128] SAGE schools are being compared to a group of 14 to 17 non-SAGE schools (the exact number depending on the year) in SAGE districts. Students are tested in reading, language arts, and math on the Comprehensive Test of Basic Skills (CTBS) Complete Battery, Terra Nova edition.

Comparison schools were selected for their similarity to one or more individual SAGE schools in demographic composition, school size, initial third-grade test scores, and percentage of low-income students. In addition to quantitative analysis, the SAGE research plan contains extensive qualitative research, including interviews of teachers and principals, surveys of teachers, examination of teacher logs, and classroom observation.

The SAGE evaluation established a baseline measure of performance for participating students by testing first-graders in the fall and the spring (beginning in 1996-97). Second-graders (beginning in 1997-98) and third-graders (beginning in 1998-99) are tested in the spring. The SAGE evaluation will track through third grade students who were first-graders in the program in 1996-97, 1997-98, and 1998-99. In any given first-grade year, the number of SAGE students with valid test scores (1,300) is somewhat smaller

---

Why Are Small Classes So Effective?

The STAR, SAGE, and other studies reviewed in this report suggest that small classes promote higher achievement for several mutually reinforcing reasons.

- Children receive more individualized instruction: one-on-one help, small-group help, class participation.
- Children misbehave less because of the family atmosphere and quick intervention by teachers.
- Teachers spend more time on direct instruction and less on classroom management.
- Classes include more "hands-on" activities, though most instruction remains teacher — not student — centered.
- Students become more actively engaged in learning than do peers in large classes.
- Teachers of small classes "burn out" less often.

than in Tennessee's STAR experiment. The control group of 850 students is substantially smaller than the combined regular-class and regular-class-with-aide groups in STAR (4,000 students). However, over the three first-grade classes as a whole, the SAGE small-classes group with valid test scores is expected to include about 4,000 students and the comparison group about 2,500.

Thus far, the SAGE evaluation has published reports for the 1996-97, 1997-98, and 1998-99 school years. The results appear consistent with those reported for the Tennessee STAR experiment. Precise comparisons must await parallel application of similar research methods to the two data sets.

- In 1996-97 and again in 1997-98, students in SAGE first-grade classrooms scored significantly higher in all areas tested. The first-grade effect sizes are in the range of 0.1 to 0.3, depending on the statistical method used.
- From spring 1997 to spring 1998, second-grade SAGE students' scores increased more than those of comparison-school students but not by statistically significant amounts (at the 0.05 level). Over the two years taken together, SAGE second-graders showed statistically significant gains in language arts, mathematics, and total score, but not in reading.
- The achievement benefit of SAGE small classes is especially strong for African-American students. In 1997-98, for example, African-American students in SAGE classes increased their average total score by 52 points compared to 33 points for African Americans in comparison schools. For whites, SAGE school first-grade test scores increased by 46 points compared to 41 in comparison schools. Thus, African-American SAGE first-grade students closed the "achievement gap" with white students over the course of the school year. However, the gap widened substantially in comparison schools.
- In 1997-98, there was no significant difference between student achievement in SAGE first-grade classes with two teachers and up to 30 students and student achievement in classes

49

with one teacher and up to 15 students. This finding held true for 1998-99 as well, suggesting that school districts that lack the resources to build new classrooms could reap the benefits of small classes by adding teachers to larger classes.

- Analyses of qualitative data suggest that teachers in SAGE classrooms have greater knowledge of each of their students, spend less time managing their classes, have more time for instruction, and use more individualized instruction.

The findings of the 1998-99 SAGE evaluation (released in January 2000) are consistent with those of the first two years. That is, on average, one can expect a small class to gain 0.2 to 0.3 standard deviations (two or three months) more than a large class in early grades. An interesting new development in the 1998-99 report was that when the achievement data of the SAGE and comparison first- and second-grade classrooms were examined over a two-year period, classrooms associated with the SAGE program consistently formed the majority of top-performing classrooms. A total of 84 first-grade classrooms (66 SAGE and 18 comparison) and 74 second-grade classrooms (60 SAGE and 14 comparison) were tracked over a two-year span. Only one first-grade comparison classroom ranked among the top 30 based on student achievement across the two years. Fourteen of the lowest-performing classrooms were from comparison schools. Of the top-performing second-grade classrooms over this period, only four were from comparison schools. Nine of the remaining 10 comparison schools fell among the 30 lowest-performing classrooms over this time span.[129]

California Initiatives

In the 1996-97 school year, California appropriated almost $11 billion to implement an ambitious class-size reduction program. In the first year, districts received $650 for each student enrolled in a class of no more than 20 students. The 1997 California budget raised the allotment to $800 per student and contained an additional $1.5 billion for class-size reduction. Schools must start by reducing class size in first grade, then in second grade, and then in either kindergarten or third grade. The program's popularity is illustrated by the fact that, by February 1997, 92% of all first-graders and 74% of all second-graders were attending small classes. By 1997-98, 873 of 895 eligible school districts were receiving aid under the program and 18,400 new classes had been added.[130]

Randy Ross, a social scientist working for school reform in Los Angeles, sharply criticized the California program for doing too much, too fast.[131] By implementing class-size reduction across the board, he claimed, the state exacerbated an existing teacher shortage. California's Legislative Analyst Office made a similar criticism:

> The CSR [class-size reduction] program result[ed] in the hiring of about 18,400 teachers [in 1996-97] in addition to the approximately 16,000 elementary teachers that will be hired for normal replacement. . . . Twenty-four percent of teachers hired for CSR are not credentialed and are working under an emergency permit or waiver. School districts rate teachers hired for CSR as being less skilled, on average, than teachers hired in previous years. At the same time districts are hiring less qualified teachers, most are also experiencing difficulties in implementing staff development for those teachers.[132]

With statewide class-size reduction, the best and most qualified teachers had their choice of districts in which to work. As some of these teachers abandoned inner-city schools, these schools hired more teachers without credentials. In Los Angeles, two-thirds of new teachers hired were without credentials.[133]

The California legislature appropriated $1.75 million for a three-year study of the impact of the class-size reduction program. The research will be conducted by a consortium of research organizations (WestEd, PACE, American Institutes for Research, RAND, and EdSource). The aim is to encourage information-sharing and learning by practitioners as well as to add to the research literature. The research design will focus on successive cohorts of third- and fourth-graders who have and have not attended smaller classes.

The first annual report, released in June 1999, found that nearly all first- and second-graders and almost two-thirds of all kindergartners and third-graders are now in reduced-size classes. The study found a small gain in achievement for all students in smaller classes, as well as higher levels of parent-teacher contact and parent satisfaction with their children's education. Unlike in the STAR studies, the consortium's examination found that all students in smaller classes demonstrated similar achievement gains, regardless of ethnicity, poverty level, or English fluency. However, the researchers also found that schools serving low-income, minority, and English-as-a-second-language students have been slower to implement the program and have experienced a greater decline in the qualifications of teachers than have other schools.[134]

CONCLUSION

→ There is no longer any argument about whether reducing class size in the primary grades increases student achievement. The research evidence is quite clear: It does.

Policy makers considering education reforms to improve the achievement of low-income children should carefully consider the strength of the evidence and the quality of the research on smaller classes. In policymaking, there is sometimes a tendency to regard all studies and research reports as being created equal. They are not. As Princeton University economist Alan Krueger put it when referring to the STAR study, "One well designed experiment should trump a phalanx of poorly controlled, imprecise observational studies based on uncertain statistical specifications."[135]

In contrast, the claim that participation in a voucher program increases student achievement remains weak. The most carefully analyzed voucher program, the Milwaukee Parental Choice Program, included a small number of students, many of whom left the program each year. Although two out of three analyses found positive achievement advantages in math (but not in reading) for voucher students, these results were derived by applying complex and sometimes controversial analytic methods to weak data. As Cecilia Rouse points out, Milwaukee Parental Choice Program data limitations threaten the validity of any evaluation of the program. Statistical techniques cannot substitute for better data.[136]

Indeed, when Rouse expanded her examination of Milwaukee student achievement data to include the city's magnet schools, regular attendance area schools, and a group of attendance area schools with small class sizes and supplemental state funding (the P-5 schools), she found that students in the P-5 schools performed as well as or better than students in choice schools. She concluded, "Given that the pupil-teacher ratios in the P-5 and choice schools are significantly smaller than those in the other public schools, one *potential* explanation for these results is that students perform well in schools with smaller class sizes" [Rouse's emphasis].[137]

Similar problems bedevil the evaluation of the Cleveland voucher program. The official evaluation of Cleveland found no significant differences between voucher and public school students in one year and gains for voucher students in only one subject, language arts, in a second year. Reminiscent of the Milwaukee evaluation debates, a team of researchers led by Paul Peterson of Harvard reexamined the official data, made two controversial methodological assumptions, and pronounced the Cleveland voucher program a success.

Faced with the ambiguity of the existing evidence, some may argue that we need more voucher experiments. This is one of the arguments being used to justify the expansion of private voucher programs described in this report; and, indeed, more reliable data may emerge in the next several years from some of these programs.

However, the problem with research on small-scale voucher experiments is not only the lack of clear performance effects. More fundamentally, the problem is that such small-scale programs — no matter how crystal clear their achievement consequences — can tell us little about larger-scale programs. Voucher evaluations are less informative than class-size research because "vouchers" do not represent a specific education reform. If a voucher program generates positive effects, the research does not generally look inside the schools to ask what explains the success. It simply assumes that private is better.

A second reason that voucher research tells education policy makers little relates to the issue of scale. As research on private schools shows, some private schools appear to raise achievement through "peer effects" — by placing low-income students with other students from more privileged families who place a high priority on education. (Elite private schools also tend to spend large amounts of money per student and to have smaller classes.) But in a large-scale voucher program, peer effects could be quite different than in a small-scale program. This may help explain why new schools that enroll voucher students in Cleveland perform less well than public schools while established private schools perform better than public schools.

For these reasons, the only way to find out the effect of a large-scale voucher program is to implement one. However, there is no strong evidence that this would improve achievement. In addition, such a large-scale program would likely raise spending on students who already attend private schools and reduce education spending on children currently in public school.

In contrast, the scholarly discussion about the academic impact of class-size reductions is largely settled as far as whether they generate benefits. What remains is a discussion about: 1) whether the achievement gained is worth the cost; 2) whether the class-size reductions should be general or targeted; and 3) how class-size reductions should be used in conjunction with other academic strategies.[138]

Despite some disagreement, there is a strong consensus that targeting class-size reductions on kindergarten and first grade will provide the greatest academic gains for the money invested. It is also widely agreed that reducing class size is a preventive strategy, not a remedial strategy. In other words, children should be taught in small classes at the earliest possible point in their school careers and reductions in class size should be used as a base on which additional education strategies are built. Thus, at a minimum, small classes in kindergarten and first grade should be seen as a strong foundation for other strategies, such as "Success for All" and "Reading Recovery," which have had good results increasing the reading achievement of low-income children.

NOTES

1. W. Van Vliet and J.A. Smyth, "A Nineteenth-Century French Proposal to Use School Vouchers," *Comparative Education Review* 26 (1982): 95-103.
2. National Commission on Excellence in Education, *A Nation at Risk: The Imperative for Educational Reform* (Washington, D.C.: U.S. Department of Education, 1983).
3. Milton Friedman, *Capitalism and Freedom* (Chicago: University of Chicago Press, 1963).
4. Jeffrey R. Henig, *Rethinking School Choice: Limits of the Market Metaphor* (Princeton, N.J.: Princeton University Press, 1993), p. 104.
5. David Tyack, *The One Best System: A History of American Urban Education* (Cambridge, Mass.: Harvard University Press, 1974).
6. Ivan Illich, *Deschooling Society* (New York: Harper & Row, 1971).
7. Allen Graubard, *Free the Children: Radical Reform and the Free School Movement* (New York: Pantheon, 1972). See also the letter from Herb Kohl to Mario Fantini printed in the appendix to Mario D. Fantini, *Free Schools of Choice* (New York: Simon and Schuster, 1973).
8. Paul Goodman, *The New Reformation: Notes of a Neolithic Conservative* (New York: Random House, 1970).
9. Christopher Jencks, *Education Vouchers: A Report on Financing Elementary Education by Grants to Parents* (Cambridge, Mass.: Center for the Study of Public Policy, 1970), as cited in Richard F. Elmore, *Choice in Public Education* (Santa Monica, Calif.: RAND Corporation, 1986), p. 9.
10. Amy Stuart Wells, *Time to Choose: America at the Crossroads of School Choice Policy* (New York: Hill and Wang, 1993), p. 152.

11. Wells, *Time to Choose*; Charles J. Russo and Michael P. Orsi, "The Supreme Court and the Breachable Wall," *Momentum* (September 1992): 42-45.

12. Thomas W. Lyons, "Parochiaid? Yes!" *Educational Leadership* (November 1971): 102-104; Glenn L. Archer, "Parochiaid? No!" *Educational Leadership* (November 1971): 105-107.

13. *Justice and Excellence: The Case for Choice in Chapter 1* (Washington, D.C.: U.S. Department of Education, 1985), as cited in Elmore, *Choice in Public Education*.

14. Henig, *Rethinking School Choice*.

15. Henig, *Rethinking School Choice*, chap. 4.

16. Education Commission of the States, "Legislative Activities Involving Open Enrollment (Choice)," *Clearinghouse Notes* (December 1994).

17. Education Commission of the States, "Legislative Activities Involving Open Enrollment (Choice)," p. 91.

18. Henig. *Rethinking School Choice*.

19. "Perspectives on Education in America: An Annotated Briefing," *Journal of Educational Research* 86, no. 5 (1993): 259-310.

20. David W. Grissmer et al., *Student Achievement and the Changing American Family* (Santa Monica, Calif.: RAND Corporation, 1994).

21. Alan B. Krueger, "Reassessing the View that American Schools Are Broken," *Economic Policy Review* (March 1998): 29-41.

22. Krueger, "Reassessing the View," p. 31.

23. Krueger, "Reassessing the View," p. 31 and Chart 2.

24. Richard Rothstein and Karen Hawley Mills, *Where's the Money Gone? Changes in the Level of Education Spending* (Washington, D.C.: Economic Policy Institute, 1995), pp. 1, 37. For an update for the 1991-96 period that shows a stagnation in spending on regular education and continued increases in special education spending, see Richard Rothstein, *Where's the Money Going? Changes in Level and Composition of Education Spending, 1991-96* (Washington, D.C.: Economic Policy Institute, 1997).

25. John E. Chubb and Terry Moe, *Politics, Markets, and America's Schools* (Washington, D.C.: Brookings Institution, 1990).

26. Chubb and Moe's work has drawn strong support and considerable criticism. In a 1995 book, Kevin J. Smith and Kenneth J. Meier analyzed Chubb and Moe's theoretical claims, methods, results, and conclusions. In addition, they reviewed data about the perfor-

mance of the school choice programs in other countries. Smith and Meier concluded that the available evidence did not support Chubb and Moe's case for vouchers. See Kevin B. Smith and Kenneth J. Meier, *The Case Against School Choice: Politics, Markets, and Fools* (Armonk, N.Y.: M.E. Sharpe, 1995).

27. 166 Wis. 2d, 501, 480 N.W.2d, 460 (1992).

28. John F. Witte, *First-Year Report: Milwaukee Parental Choice Program* (Madison: Robert M. LaFollette Institute of Public Affairs, University of Wisconsin-Madison, 1991); John F. Witte, Andrea B. Bailey, and Christopher A. Thorn, *Second-Year Report: Milwaukee Parental Choice Program* (Madison: Robert M. LaFollette Institute of Public Affairs, University of Wisconsin-Madison, 1992); John F. Witte, Andrea B. Bailey, and Christopher A. Thorn, *Third-Year Report: Milwaukee Parental Choice Program* (Madison: Robert M. LaFollette Institute of Public Affairs, University of Wisconsin-Madison, 1993); John F. Witte et al., *Fourth-Year Report: Milwaukee Parental Choice Program* (Madison: Robert M. LaFollette Institute of Public Affairs, University of Wisconsin-Madison, 1994); John F. Witte, Troy D. Sterr, and Christopher A. Thorn, *Fifth-Year Report: Milwaukee Parental Choice Program* (Madison: Robert M. LaFollette Institute of Public Affairs, University of Wisconsin-Madison, 1995).

29. Paul E. Peterson, *A Critique of the Witte Evaluation of Milwaukee's School Choice Program* (Cambridge, Mass.: Harvard University Center for American Political Studies, 1995).

30. George A. Mitchell, *The Milwaukee Parental Choice Program* (Milwaukee: Wisconsin Policy Research Institute, 1992); John E. Chubb and Terry M. Moe, *Educational Choice: Answers to the Most Frequently Asked Questions About Mediocrity in American Education and What Can Be Done About It* (Milwaukee: Wisconsin Policy Research Institute, 1989).

31. Wisconsin Legislative Audit Bureau, *Milwaukee Parental Choice Program* (Madison, 1995).

32. Witte, *First-Year Report: Milwaukee Parental Choice Program*; Witte, Bailey, and Thorn, *Second-Year Report: Milwaukee Parental Choice Program*; Witte, Bailey, and Thorn, *Third-Year Report: Milwaukee Parental Choice Program*; Witte et al., *Fourth-Year Report: Milwaukee Parental Choice Program*; Witte, Sterr, and Thorn, *Fifth-Year Report: Milwaukee Parental Choice Program*.

33. John F. Witte, "Achievement Effects of the Milwaukee Voucher Program" (Paper presented at the American Economics Association Annual Meeting, New Orleans, 4-6 January 1997); John F. Witte, "The Milwaukee Voucher Experiment," *Educational Evaluation and Policy Analysis* 20, no. 4 (1998): 229-51.

34. Jay P. Greene, Paul E. Peterson, and Jiangtao Du, *The Effectiveness of School Choice in Milwaukee: A Secondary Analysis of Data from the Program's Evaluation* (Cambridge, Mass.: Program in Education Policy and Governance, Harvard University, 1996). Jay P. Greene, Paul E. Peterson, and Jiangtao Du, *Effectiveness of School Choice: The Milwaukee Experiment* (Cambridge, Mass.: Program in Education Policy and Governance, Harvard University, 1997).

35. Cecilia Rouse, "Private School Vouchers and Student Achievement: An Evaluation of the Milwaukee Parental Choice Program," *Quarterly Journal of Economics* 113, no. 2 (1998): 553-602. Cecilia Elena Rouse, "Schools and Student Achievement: More Evidence from the Milwaukee Parental Choice Program (Revised Edition)," *Princeton University Industrial Relations Bulletin No. 396* (Princeton, N.J.: Princeton University and National Bureau of Economic Research, 1998), available at http://www.irs.princeton.edu/pubs/working_papers.html.

36. Wisconsin Legislative Audit Bureau, *Milwaukee Parental Choice Program*.

37. Wisconsin Legislative Audit Bureau, *Milwaukee Parental Choice Program*.

38. Wisconsin DPI School Management Services, "Milwaukee Parental Choice Program Membership and Payment History, in Total, 1990 to Present," Table, available from http://www.dpi.state.wi.us/dpi/dfm/sms/histmem.html.

39. Ken Black, Milwaukee Public Schools Senior Budget Analyst, telephone interview, 19 December 1997.

40. Brent Staples, "Schoolyard Brawl: The New Politics of Education Casts Blacks in Starring Role," *New York Times*, 4 January 1998, p. 49.

41. Greene, Peterson, and Du, *The Effectiveness of School Choice in Milwaukee*.

42. Witte et al., *Fourth-Year Report: Milwaukee Parental Choice Program*.

43. Rouse, *Schools and Student Achievement: More Evidence from the Milwaukee Parental Choice Program*.

44. The description of the Cleveland Scholarship and Tutoring Program is based on documents provided by the Ohio Department of Education; discussions with Francis Rogers of the Ohio Department of Education and Bert Holt of the Cleveland Scholarship and Tutoring Program; and Dan Murphy, F. Howard Nelson, and Bella Rosenberg, *The Cleveland Voucher Program: Who Chooses? Who Gets Chosen? Who Pays?* (Washington, D.C.: American Federation of Teachers, 1997).

45. Nina Shokraii Rees and Sarah E. Youssef, *School Choice: What's Happening in the States, 1999* (Heritage Foundation, 3 September 1999); http://www.heritage.org/schools/ohio.html.

46. Rees and Youssef, *School Choice*.

47. Paul E. Peterson, Jay P. Greene, and William Howell, *New Findings from the Cleveland Scholarship Program: A Reanalysis of Data from the Indiana University School of Education Evaluation* (Cambridge, Mass.: Program on Education Policy and Governance, Harvard University, 1998).

48. Kim K. Metcalf et al., *A Comparative Evaluation of the Cleveland Scholarship and Tutoring Program: Year One, 1996-97* (Bloomington: Indiana Center for Evaluation, Indiana University, 1998); Kim K. Metcalf et al., *Evaluation of the Cleveland Scholarship and Tutoring Program: Second-Year Report, 1997-98* (Bloomington: Indiana Center for Evaluation, Indiana University, 1998).

49. Peterson, Greene, and Howell, *New Findings*, p. 4.

50. David N. Figlio and Joe A. Stone, *School Choice and Student Performance: Are Private Schools Really Better?* (Madison: Institute for Research on Poverty, University of Wisconsin-Madison, 1997).

51. Maureen Wahl, *First-Year Report of the Partners Advancing Values in Education Scholarship Program* (Milwaukee: Family Service America, 1993); Maureen Wahl, *Second-Year Report of the Partners Advancing Values in Education Scholarship Program* (Milwaukee: Family Service America, 1994); Maureen Wahl, *Third-Year Report of the Partners Advancing Values in Education* (Milwaukee: Family Service America, 1995); Sammis B. White, Peter Maier, and Christine Cramer, *Fourth-Year Report of the Partners Advancing Values in Education Scholarship Program* (Milwaukee: Urban Research Center, University of Wisconsin-Milwaukee, 1996).

52. David J. Weinschrott and Sally B. Kilgore, *Educational Choice Charitable Trust: An Experiment in School Choice* (Washington, D.C.: Hudson Institute, 1996).

53. Paul E. Peterson et al., *Initial Findings from the Evaluation of the New York School Choice Scholarships Program* (Cambridge, Mass.: Mathematica Policy Research and Harvard University Program on Education Policy and Governance, 1997).

54. Paul E. Peterson, David Myers, and William G. Howell, *An Evaluation of the New York School Choice Scholarships Program: The First Year* (Cambridge, Mass.: Mathematica Policy Research and Harvard University Program on Education Policy and Governance, 1998).

55. This statistical method, a "one-tailed test," is an uncommon test of significance, usually used when there are strong theoretical reasons for believing that the change in the independent variable (in this case, attendance at Choice schools) is likely to produce a change in the dependent variable (test scores) in only one direction. In the Greene, Peterson, and Du analysis, the assumption was made that Choice students could not perform worse on tests than those who applied to the program but were rejected (that is, that only one direction of change, improvement, was possible for Choice students).

56. Greene, Peterson, and Du, *The Effectiveness of School Choice in Milwaukee*.

57. Peterson, Myers, and Howell, *An Evaluation of the New York School Choice Scholarships Program*, p. 32.

58. C.M. Achilles, Letter to the Editor, *Education Week*, 12 January 1999.

59. See Paul E. Peterson, Jay P. Greene, and William G. Howell, "Initial Findings from an Evaluation of School Choice Programs in Washington, D.C." (Paper presented at the Annual Meeting of the American Political Science Association, Boston, September 1998); Paul E. Peterson et al., "Initial Findings from an Evaluation of School Choice Programs in Washington, D.C., and Dayton, Ohio" (Paper presented at the Annual Meeting of the Association for Public Policy Analysis and Management, New York, October 1998).

60. R. Kenneth Godwin, Frank R. Kemerer, and Valerie J. Martinez, "Comparing Public Choice and Private Voucher Programs in San

Antonio," in *Learning from School Choice*, edited by Paul E. Peterson and Bryan C. Hassel (Washington, D.C.: Brookings Institution Press, 1998), pp. 275-306.

61. Robert B. Aguirre, *A Report on the First Semester of the Horizon Voucher Program* (San Antonio: CEO America Foundation, 1999).

62. Peter W. Cookson, *School Choice: The Struggle for the Soul of American Education* (New Haven, Conn.: Yale University Press, 1994); Jeffrey R. Henig, *Rethinking School Choice: Limits of the Market Metaphor* (Princeton, N.J.: Princeton University Press, 1993).

63. Henry M. Levin, "Educational Vouchers: Effectiveness, Choice, and Costs," *Journal of Policy Analysis and Management* 17, no. 3 (1998): 373-92.

64. Casey D. Cobb and Gene V. Glass, "Ethnic Segregation in Arizona Charter Schools," *Education Policy Analysis Archives* 7, no. 1 (1999). http://epaa.asu.edu/epaa/v7n1.

65. David Arsen, David Plank, and Gary Sykes, *School Choice Policies in Michigan: The Rules Matter* (East Lansing: Michigan State University Educational Policy Center, 1999). http://edtech.connect. msu.edu/choice.

66. Godwin, Kemerer, and Martinez, "Comparing Public Choice and Private Voucher Programs in San Antonio," pp. 275-306.

67. Carnegie Foundation for the Advancement of Teaching, *School Choice: A Special Report.* (Princeton, N.J., 1992).

68. Bruce Fuller, *Who Gains, Who Loses from School Choice: A Research Summary* (Denver: National Conference of State Legislatures, 1995).

69. Geoff Whitty, "Creating Quasi-Markets in Education: A Review of Recent Research on Parental Choice and School Autonomy in Three Countries," in *Review of Research in Education*, edited by Michael W. Apple (Washington, D.C.: American Educational Research Association, 1997); Martin Carnoy, "Is School Privatization the Answer? Data from the Experience of Other Countries Suggest Not," *Education Week*, 12 July 1995, p. 52.

70. Terry Moe, ed. *Private Vouchers* (Stanford, Calif.: Hoover Institution Press, 1995).

71. Moe, *Private Vouchers.*

72. Derrick Z. Jackson, "The Corruption of School Choice," *Boston Globe*, 28 October 1998, A23.

73. Glen E. Robinson and James H. Wittebols, *Class Size Research: A Related Cluster Analysis for Decision Making* (Arlington, Va.: Educational Research Service, 1986).

74. Douglas Mitchell, Cristi Carson, and Gary Badarak, *How Changing Class Size Affects Classrooms and Students* (Riverside: California Educational Research Cooperative, University of California-Riverside, 1989).

75. Robinson and Wittebols, *Class Size Research.*

76. Mitchell, Carson, and Badarak, *How Changing Class Size Affects Classrooms and Students.*

77. Gene V. Glass and Mary Lee Smith, *Meta-Analysis of Research on the Relationship of Class-Size and Achievement* (San Francisco: Far West Laboratory for Educational Research and Development, 1978). See also Gene V. Glass et al. *School Class Size: Research and Policy* (Beverly Hills, Calif.: Sage, 1982).

78. Robinson and Wittebols, *Class Size Research.*

79. Robert E. Slavin, "Meta-Analysis in Education: How Has It Been Used?" *Educational Researcher* 13, no. 8 (1984): 6-15, 24-27.

80. For a current synopsis of Prime Time, see Indiana Department of Education, "Prime Time: An Overview," no date, available from the Prime Time office by calling 317-232-9163.

81. David Gilman and Christopher Tillitski, "The Longitudinal Effects of Smaller Classes: Four Studies," October 1990, ERIC Document Reproduction Service No. ED 326 313.

82. B. Farr et al., *Evaluation of Prime Time: 1986-87, Final Report* (Indianapolis, Ind.: Advanced Technology, no date); Mary Quilling, Linda Parker, and David Gray, "Prime Time: Six Years Later" (Prepared for the Indiana Department of Education by PRC, 1992).

83. Quilling, Parker, and Gray, "Prime Time," p. 20.

84. Quilling, Parker, and Gray, "Prime Time," p. 25.

85. Quilling, Parker, and Gray, "Prime Time," p. 29.

86. Helen Pate-Bain et al., "Class Size Reduction in Metro Nashville: A Three-Year Cohort Study," *ERS Spectrum* 6, no. 4 (1988): 30-36.

87. Jayne Boyd-Zaharias and Helen Pate-Bain, *Teacher Aides and Student Learning: Lessons from Project STAR* (Arlington, Va.: Educational Research Service, 1998).

88. Elizabeth Word et al., *Student/Teacher Achievement Ratio (STAR): Tennessee's K-3 Class Size Study, Final Summary Report 1985-1990* (Nashville: Tennessee Department of Education, 1990).

89. Alan B. Krueger, "Experimental Estimates of Education Production Functions," *Quarterly Journal of Economics* 114, no. 2 (1999): 497-532.

90. Jayne Boyd-Zaharias et al., "Quality Schools Build On a Quality Start," in *Creating the Quality School*, edited by Edward W. Chance (Madison, Wis.: Magna Publications, 1995). In regression analysis, Alan Krueger also considered the impact of using actual class size rather than the original designations into small and regular classes. As in the Boyd-Zaharias study, having a class-size difference of more than 10 generates a significantly larger effect size than when considering the originally designated small and regular classes as a group. Krueger, "Experimental Estimates."

91. Elizabeth Word et al., *Student/Teacher Achievement Ratio (STAR)*. These findings are also reported in Jeremy D. Finn et al., "Three Years in a Small Class," *Teaching and Teacher Education* 6, no. 2 (1990): 127-36.

92. Jeremy D. Finn and Charles M. Achilles, "Tennessee's Class Size Study: Findings, Implications, Misconceptions," *Educational Evaluation and Policy Analysis* 21, no. 2 (1999): 97-109. Emphasis in original. See also Jeremy D. Finn and Charles M. Achilles, "Answers and Questions About Class Size: A Statewide Experiment," *American Educational Research Journal* 27, no. 3 (1990): 557-77.

93. Alan B. Krueger, "Experimental Estimates."

94. Charles M. Achilles, Jeremy D. Finn, and Helen P. Bain, "Using Class Size to Reduce the Equity Gap," *Educational Leadership* 55, no. 4 (1997): 40-43.

95. C. Steven Bingham. *White-Minority Achievement Gap Reduction and Small Class Size: A Research and Literature Review* (Nashville: Center of Excellence for Research and Policy on Basic Skills, Tennessee State University, 1993).

96. John Folger and Carolyn Breda, "Evidence from Project STAR About Class Size and Student Achievement," *Peabody Journal of Education* 67, no. 1 (1989): 17-33.

97. W.J. Fowler Jr. and J. Walberg, "School Size, Characteristics and Outcomes," *Educational Evaluation and Policy Analysis* 13, no. 2 (1991): 189-202.

98. Charles M. Achilles, *Summary of Recent Class-Size Research with an Emphasis on Tennessee's Project STAR and Its Derivative Re-*

search Studies (Nashville: Center of Excellence for Research and Policy on Basic Skills, no date).

99. Frederick Mosteller, "The Tennessee Study of Class Size in the Early School Grades," *The Future of Children* 5, no. 2 (1995): 113-27.

100. Eric A. Hanushek, *The Evidence on Class Size* (Rochester, N.Y.: W. Allen Wallis Institute of Political Economy, University of Rochester, 1998).

101. Alan B. Krueger, "Experimental Estimates of Education Production Functions," *Quarterly Journal of Economics* 114, no. 2 (1999): 497-532.

102. The LBS follow-up to STAR led to the establishment of a statewide K-3 class-size reduction in 1995. Under this reduction, Tennessee provided state funding to reduce K-3 class size to 20 statewide with an option of 15 for at-risk students. These goals are expected to be achieved by the year 2001 and are already 80% achieved in kindergarten and grade one. The STAR and LBS projects and subsequent legislative action are excellent examples of the effective use of research and evaluation by state policy makers.

103. In the eighth-grade technical report, about half the sample had been in small K-3 classes. About 20% of the sample had only one year in a small class. Barbara A. Nye et al., *The Lasting Benefits Study, Eighth Grade Technical Report* (Nashville: Center of Excellence for Research in Basic Skills, 1995), Table 1, p. 5.

104. Nye et al., *The Lasting Benefits Study, Eighth Grade.* See also Barbara A. Nye, "Class Size and School Effectiveness: Answers from Longitudinal Studies" (Paper presented at the 11th International Congress for School Effectiveness and School Improvement, University of Manchester, U.K., January 1998).

105. Barbara A. Nye et al., *The Lasting Benefits Study, Fourth Grade Technical Report* (Nashville: Center of Excellence for Research in Basic Skills, Tennessee State University, 1991).

106. Nye et al., *The Lasting Benefits Study, Eighth Grade*, Tables 5 and 7.

107. Nye, "Class Size and School Effectiveness."

108. Barbara A. Nye et al., *The Lasting Benefits Study: Seventh Grade Technical Report* (Nashville: Center of Excellence for Research in Basic Skills, Tennessee State University, 1994).

109. Barbara A. Nye et al., *The Lasting Benefits Study, Sixth Grade Technical Report* (Nashville: Center of Excellence for Research

in Basic Skills, Tennessee State University, 1993).

110. Barbara A. Nye, B. DeWayne Fulton, and Jayne Boyd-Zaharias, *The Lasting Benefits Study, Fifth Grade Technical Report* (Nashville: Center of Excellence for Research in Basic Skills, Tennessee State University, 1992).

111. Barbara Nye, Larry V. Hedges, and Spyros Konstantopoulos, "The Long-Term Effects of Small Classes: A Five-Year Follow-Up of the Tennessee Class Size Experiment," *Educational Evaluation and Policy Analysis* 21, no. 2 (1999): 127-42, especially Table 5. The authors caution that the assignment of students to the groups that received one, two, three, and four years of small classes was not random because students' moves into and out of STAR classrooms were controlled by parents' decisions about moving. If students who moved into or out of STAR classrooms during the experiment differed systematically from students who remained in the classrooms the entire time, this could distort the results.

112. David W. Grissmer, "Class Size Effects: Assessing the Evidence, Its Policy Implications, and Future Research Agenda," *Educational Evaluation and Policy Analysis* 21, no. 2 (1999): 231-48.

113. Grissmer, "Class Size Effects," pp. 97-109.

114. Grissmer, "Class Size Effects."

115. Grissmer, "Class Size Effects."

116. Helen Pate-Bain et al., *The Student/Teacher Achievement Ratio (STAR) Project: STAR Follow-Up Studies 1996-1997* (Lebanon, Tenn.: Health and Education Research Operative Services, 1997).

117. Alan B. Krueger and Diane M. Whitmore, "The Effects of Attending a Small Class in the Early Grades on College Attendance Plans" (Princeton University, 9 April 1998).

118. Helen Pate-Bain, B. DeWayne Fulton, and Jayne Boyd-Zaharias, *Effects of Class-Size Reduction in the Early Grades (K-3) on High School Performance* (Lebanon, Tenn.: Health and Education Research Operative Services, 1999).

119. Barbara A. Nye et al., *Project Challenge: Fifth Year Summary Report* (Nashville: Center of Excellence for Research in Basic Skills, Tennessee State University, 1995). See also the first (1991), second (1992), and third (1993) Project Challenge summary reports, and Charles M. Achilles et al., "The Lasting Benefits Study (LBS) in Grades 4 and 5 (1990-1991): A Legacy from Tennessee's Four-Year (K-3) Class-Size Study (1985-1989),

Project STAR" (Paper presented at the North Carolina Association for Research in Education, Greensboro, 14 January 1993).

120. For data on class size in Nevada K-3 classrooms over time, see H. Pepper Sturm, *Nevada's Class-Size Reduction Program* (Carson City: Senate Human Resources Committee, Nevada Legislative Counsel Bureau, 1997).

121. Mary Snow, telephone interview, 14 January 1998.

122. Mary Snow, *An Evaluation of the Class Size Reduction Program* (Carson City: Nevada Department of Education, 1999).

123. Mary Snow, *An Evaluation of the Class Size Reduction Program* (Carson City: Nevada Department of Education, 1998).

124. Mary Snow, *An Evaluation of the Class Size Reduction Program* (Carson City: Nevada Department of Education, 1997), pp. 3, 5.

125. James Pollard and Kim Yap, *The Nevada Class Size Reduction Evaluation Study, 1995* (Carson City: Nevada Department of Education, 1995).

126. Judith S. Costa and Rhoton Hudson, "Report Prepared by Testing and Evaluation Department," Clark County School District, February 1995, p. 5.

127. The term "student-teacher ratio" is used here because a number of participating schools reduced their class sizes by means other than placing one teacher with 15 students. In the SAGE program, "student-teacher ratio" is used in ways that capture the everyday understanding of "class size." For example, it is not a statistical artifact of having many certified staff members outside the classroom.

128. Peter Maier et al., *First-Year Results of the Student Achievement Guarantee in Education Program* (Milwaukee: Center for Urban Initiatives and Research, University of Wisconsin-Milwaukee, 1997); Alex Molnar, Philip Smith, and John Zahorik, *1997-98 Evaluation Results of the Student Achievement Guarantee in Education (SAGE) Program* (Milwaukee: School of Education, University of Wisconsin-Milwaukee, 1998). These documents are available on the SAGE website (http://www.uwm.edu/Dept/CERAI/sage.html). See also Alex Molnar, Philip Smith, and John Zahorik, "Evaluating the SAGE Program: A Pilot Program in Targeted Pupil-Teacher Reduction in Wisconsin," *Educational Evaluation and Policy Analysis* 21, no. 2 (1999): 165-77.

129. Alex Molnar, Philip Smith, and John Zahorik, et al., *1998-99 Evaluation of the Student Achievement Guarantee in Education (SAGE) Program* (Milwaukee: Center for Education Research,

Analysis, and Innovation, University of Wisconsin-Milwaukee, 1999).

130. Data for 1996-97 come from http://www.lao.ca.gov/class_ size_297.html. Data for 1997-98 are from Edward Wexler et al., *California's Class Size Reduction: Implications for Equity, Practice, and Implementation* (San Francisco: PACE-WestEd, 1998).

131. Randy Ross, "The Dark Secret Behind California's Class Size Reduction Program," *Education Week*, 17 May 1999. Cited in Richard Rothstein, "Small Classes Make a Big Difference. . . Ceteris Paribus," http://www.prospect.org/columns/rothstein/ Rothstein0599.html.

132. California Legislative Analyst's Office, "Class Size Reduction," 12 February 1997. http://www.lao.ca.gov/class_size_297.html.

133. Rothstein, "Small Classes Make a Big Difference."

134. Brian M. Stecher and George W. Bohrnstedt, *Class Size Reduction in California: Early Evaluation Findings, 1996-98* (Palo Alto, Calif.: CSR Research Consortium, 1999).

135. Krueger, "Experimental Estimates of Education Production Functions."

136. Rouse, *Schools and Student Achievement: More Evidence from the Milwaukee Parental Choice Program.*

137. Rouse, *Schools and Student Achievement: More Evidence from the Milwaukee Parental Choice Program.*

138. Robinson and Wittebols, *Class Size Research.*

ABOUT THE AUTHOR

Alex Molnar holds a Ph.D. in urban education and has been a professor in the School of Education at the University of Wisconsin-Milwaukee since 1972. Previously he taught high school social studies in the Chicago area. From 1993 to 1995, Molnar served as chief of staff for the Wisconsin Department of Public Instruction Urban Initiative. Currently he is a member of the legislatively mandated evaluation team for the Wisconsin small schools initiative, the Student Achievement Guarantee in Education (SAGE).

Molnar has edited, written, and co-authored a number of books, including *Changing Problem Behavior in Schools* (Jossey-Bass, 1989), which is used widely by American educators and has been translated into four languages. Molnar also consults extensively with school districts throughout the United States.